The
Predictability
Factor

The Predictability Factor

DR. BILL AGEE

Library of Congress Control Number:		2015907496
ISBN:	Hardcover	978-1-5035-7003-0
	Softcover	978-1-5035-7002-3
	eBook	978-1-5035-7001-6

Rev. date: 05/18/2015

To order additional copies of this book, contact:
Xlibris
1-888-795-4274
www.Xlibris.com
Orders@Xlibris.com
712094

CONTENTS

I dedicate this work to my wife and my family, who continually inspire and challenge me to go beyond what I believe I am capable of and achieve things I never thought possible.

FOREWORD

My friend and co-laborer, Dr. Bill Agee, has written a masterpiece to aid in the success of church planting and church revitalization. *"The Predictability Factor"*, was written from Dr. Agee's years of experience in this field of ministry. He is a seasoned practitioner and has been an incredible asset to the ministry of First Baptist Church, Woodstock. If you have a desire to see a church birthed or revitalized this book will give you great insight into how to make it happen.

Dr. Johnny Hunt

ACKNOWLEDGMENTS

I want to acknowledge the tireless and self-less church planters and church revitalization pastors who serve often in anonymity, without recognition for their sacrifice. These men and their families make a tremendous difference in the expansion of God's kingdom around the world. To all who are currently serving or will serve in the future, you have my unreserved respect and gratitude for all you do.

INTRODUCTION

Church planting has seen a dramatic shift in both its prominence and importance over the past few decades. In the late 1970s and early 1980s, church planting was hardly on the horizon and certainly not mainstream. Occasionally a person would strike out on his own to start a new *"mission."* Little was known about how to start a new church and see it become successful.

The new "missions" were not talked about much, and when they were, it was more in a negative tone, by pastors who feared the new "mission" might take some of their members away. While many attitudes have changed over the years, the idea that new churches are a threat to existing churches remains to this day, but the concept of partnership has made a tremendous difference in the last few years to dispel the fear of new churches.

In the past several decades, church planting has achieved a new level of visibility for my lifetime. More training is available than ever before, more resources are available than ever before, and more partners are available than ever before, yet the success rate of new churches has changed minimally from decades earlier. It would appear that the degree of correlation between additional training and additional partnership, resulting in greater church planting success, is not as anticipated.

The Question Is, Why?

Why is it not possible to predict future success of church plants in a significant way? Why is it not possible to know what leads to an enhanced predictability of success? Why do new churches still fail at an alarming rate, with no real ability to change the results? Why is it not possible to turn the failure percentage around to a success percentage?

Perhaps Another Question Should Be Asked

What if it were possible to do all the things listed above? What if it were possible to greatly enhance the predictability of success in church plants? Would that mean an expansion of God's kingdom? Would that mean more people saved and serving the Lord? Would that not encourage churches to get involved in such a relevant and exciting work of God?

I believe it would.

This book has been in my heart for a long time. However, without the evidence to support the premise that it is possible to enhance the predictability of future success of church plants, the book was not written.

I believe it is possible to enhance predictability. I have seen it and experienced it. Now the evidence can support the premise. This book is from my heart but also from my experience. God has shown a degree of his favor on the ministry to which he called me and allowed a significant number of successful new churches to be birthed, though a few were unsuccessful.

I want to share some of the journey to which God has called me and my wife. Part of that sense of calling has led us to this time in our ministry to write this book. My first book, *"Church Planting: This is NOT a Manual"*, was to point out that church planting is more of a lifestyle based on a calling than a manual to follow. This book also is not intended to be a manual. It is a collection of God moments over-time that have been born out of experience and trust in God. Whether or not this premise is true for anyone else, it has been true in my ministry.

I hope this book provides encouragement for people to risk knowing that God is there and in total control. I hope this book challenges pastors to bring new life into the world through new churches. I hope this book becomes a source of processes and protocols leading to new churches making a kingdom difference in the world. I hope this book challenges the status quo and leads to church planters considering the possibility of church plants succeeding and flourishing as the standard, not the exception. Basically, I hope this book changes the way people think about planting a church.

Church Revitalization

I also hope this book provides encouragement to pastors of churches who, for longer than they care to admit, have lost their way. Their church is no longer in a position to effectively minister the Good News in the neighborhood or region where it is located. There is no clearly defined vision of where the church needs to be one, two, five years down the road. Yet, the pastor wants to see it turn around.

The church did not come to this position over-night. It was a process. Much like when a person attends a movie. When the person first walks in, he cannot see anything, but after a while, his eyes adjust and he gets used to the dark. That is what can happen in church. Over time, people can get used to the dark. The key components discovered through a research project and identified in this book, which lead to enhanced predictability of success of church plants, also apply to churches in need of revitalization.

Several years ago, a song was recorded and used this phrase several times, "I hope you get the chance to live like you were dying." The churches in need of revitalization have lost the urgency to live with the end in mind. What would be different in your life if you knew you were dying? What would be important now that was not important yesterday?

Some pastors preside over churches with assets but with no man-power or direction to utilize them for the good of the kingdom Just a few people are left, and their offerings do not even pay the bills, much less carry out a global evangelism ministry. The pastor wants to see it live on and make a kingdom difference but struggles to determine what must be done to see the church alive again.

Pastors of churches in need of revitalization feel they have done all they know, but nothing has changed. They have prayed more than ever before, yet nothing has happened. They have fired all the spiritual bullets in their gun, and the enemy lives on.

A number of pastors of churches in the process of church revitalization have now arrived at a place where they are tired and realize they are not the person God will use to turn the church around, yet they still want to see it live on. They are looking for another church to take the reins and cast a fresh vision. They are looking for a magic bullet . . . but none exists.

Still, other pastors are sensing a call from God to step into the leadership role in a church in need of revitalization. What does that call mean in reality? What is it a call to do? Certainly it is not a call to business as usual nor is it a call to destroy the heritage of a once-vibrant church. Knowing and assembling the key components identified in this book can have a dramatic effect on the future of the church.

Things to Consider

As a revitalization pastor, you will not be the typical pastor of a typical Baptist Church, with all the trappings that accompany the role. If that is your desire, there are already thousands of existing churches needing pastors.

- It is more than likely that the typical and mundane have brought the church into a need for revitalization in the first place.

- To attempt to keep alive and reproduce the programs and ministries utilized in the past, even in the glory days, will be a grave mistake.

- Scripture teaches us that one of the worst things that can happen is for new wine to be put into old wine-skins. Inevitably, both will be destroyed. To even think of doing the leadership role with the same mind-set and practice used in a typical church would spell disaster for all involved.

- As a revitalization pastor, you will be required to think and serve with a completely different set of parameters than a person entering a pastoral role.

- As a revitalization pastor, you will be as close to a church planter as possible. The situation you will find will be one similar to that of a missionary.

- Church planters and missionaries must start from nothing and begin to think with the end in mind. There are few, if any, systems to oversee. Everything that comes forth will come from a fresh eye, based on a fresh vision.

- As a revitalization pastor, you will be required to see things differently than you did in the past.

- As a revitalization pastor, you will need to see your neighbors and the nations with a "whatever-it-takes" mentality, not only on some issues, but on every issue.

- As a revitalization pastor, you will need a "whatever-it-takes" mentality regarding outreach and evangelism. The few people you may have to begin with may not be the ones you will need to build the church. They are still tied to a church process that is dying.

There must be a sense of urgency on the part of the revitalization pastor to identify the church's neighbors, engage them intentionally, and begin to find ways to reach them. To fail to do whatever it takes to reach new people is to seal the fate of the church. Nothing can be of more importance than reaching new people for Christ.

Pastoring a church in the process of revitalization means evangelism is at the top of the priority list. If the pastor and leaders do not see reaching people as a prime directive from God for the church, they should not pursue leading through revitalization. If the pastor thinks preaching is his gift-set, then by all means, go preach somewhere, but to be a pastor of a church in the process of revitalization is to be an evangelist first and always. The urgency never goes away.

Along with a whatever-it-takes mentality and a commitment to urgent evangelism, the pastor will need to determine ways to engage new people. Many of us grew up in Beaver Cleaver world, where there was a great deal of sameness. To think and serve like a church planter and a missionary with the end in mind means the pastor and leaders will need to understand that every person is uniquely different and will need to be engaged in many different ways. What has been done in a former ministry, although successful, will not suffice in a revitalization situation.

The revitalization pastor must practice exegesis of his context and culture, much as a church planter or missionary would study the context into which they were placed. This new entity, called a church in revitalization, has not been engaged with and has a very unique set of issues with which most ministers will not be familiar. Questions must be asked, people must be interviewed, situations must be understood, and value systems must be analyzed before the pastor will know the best ways to engage the people who now have become his field of ministry.

There is no manual here. This is the pastor and God trying to understand who it is he is trying to reach and what the best way to reach them may be. This cannot be done from an office. This is field-work.

In a church in revitalization, there must be no encumbrances, either good or bad. Forget former successes and former failures. The revitalization pastor must now depend on what God teaches him without relying on his former successes in ministry.

The revitalization pastor will need to approach this new role with a clear understanding that a singular approach will not work. There must be multiple facets to the ministry to touch as many as possible. A church planter or missionary living with the end in mind, with a sense of urgency, and a whatever-it-takes mentality, would see people in the area around the church in revitalization as lonely, spiritually destitute, and in need of a loving and caring relationship with someone who cares for them.

Very little of the role of the leader of a church in revitalization would bear resemblance to that of a typical pastor. In this role, the pastor becomes the instigator, entrepreneur, starter, motivator, visionary, and relationship builder. These are qualities often found missing in churches in need of revitalization. They have had the chaplain, studier, hand-holder, and referee. They need a pastor to be something other than what they have had at this point.

As the visionary, the revitalization pastor has the opportunity to give the people a future picture of what the church can be and how they can play a role in its growth and development. The pastor must help the people see what things are important and what things are not. The pastor must lead the people to execute well those things that are priorities and not waste energy and time on things that will not make a kingdom difference.

The dynamics of planting a church and leading a church in revitalization are very similar. I have used the principles laid out in this book in multitudes of church planting situations and church revitalization situations, with a high measure of success in both. I hope the identification of the key components, the "Count the Cost" process, and the lessons described in this book will be beneficial to church planters, sending and partnering churches, and pastors in churches needing revitalization.

PART ONE
The Research Project

CHAPTER ONE

The Predictability Factor:
In the Beginning

I was born and spent my early years in Northeastern Oklahoma, in an area known for producing tornadoes, so much so that it was called, "Tornado Alley." Almost like clock-work, every spring the local weatherman would interrupt my favorite television programs with this announcement, "Conditions are favorable for severe storms to develop in the following counties." The weatherman would then proceed to list the counties forecasted to develop and produce the severe storms. After a very short time, he would interrupt the program again to report on the severe storms that had developed exactly where he said they would develop.

I would often wonder as a child, *How did he know the location of the developing storms? How could he predict what was about to happen with such a great degree of accuracy?* My curiosity was awakened, and predictability became a topic that absorbed all my free time and energy.

Early Fascination with Predictability

Over the years, I became fascinated with the concept of weather, but also predictability in all facets of life. I read books, did research, and spent as much time as possible observing weather conditions. I also learned how the weatherman knew where the severe storms would develop.

It seems, if certain elements in the atmosphere are present and are given time to interact, predictable results are possible. The key to an effective and accurate forecast rests in identifying the key elements necessary to produce predictable results. Without the knowledge of the key elements and how they interact, forecasting will be nothing more than guess-work.

My fascination intensified into a life-long passion. I found myself driving to locations to watch the development of storms, remembering that certain elements interacting together produced the storms in a specific location. In fact, as of the writing of this book, I am involved in a tornado chasing tour and have already engaged with multiple tornadoes on the trip.

The conditions and elements present in the atmosphere indicate to the meteorologists leading the tour where the best locations are for the development of severe storms. The degree of accuracy is uncanny. Everything I am experiencing on this tour gives greater credibility to the concept of predictability.

In each of the places I have lived, the weather required a different set of components to come together and interact with other components to produce tornadoes in the Mid-west, blizzards in the northern plains, the monsoon in Arizona, and ice storms in Georgia. For a forecast to be made regarding any of these phenomenon and then to see it come to fruition is an exciting thing. I then wondered if the desire for enhanced predictability extended past the weather. My curiosity was once again engaged, and an answer had to be found.

The ability to enhance the predictability of something with a significant degree of accuracy is sought after and desired in virtually every aspect of life. Businesses seek ways to predict success for their clients. Meteorologists seek ways to predict where and when severe weather may occur to ensure safety of their viewers. By understanding dew-points, wind velocity, humidity, and many other components forecasters can increase their accuracy of the forecast. Geologists seek to understand more about earthquakes to better predict when and where one may occur, allowing people to move out of the danger zone.

Churches in revitalization, and especially church plants seek to identify what components are necessary to enhance future success, helping to bring as many people into the kingdom of God as possible. Revitalization pastors seek to know and understand the components of success so their church can be effective once more. Predictability has a much wider range than one would imagine.

Predictability Is All Around Us

Predictability is not something that only applies to one area of life or one field of study. The potential for enhanced predictability is all around us. In nature, there is a clear predictability factor. Each watermelon has an even number of stripes. Snowflakes, although extremely unique, always have six sides. Humans have twenty-three pairs of chromosomes. Add one or delete one and something completely different is formed. In sports, athletes practice so they have a greater degree of predictability of a great shot or a great play when the opportunity presents itself.

As a minister of the gospel and, in particular, a facilitator of church planting and church revitalization, I am faced with this ageless question: "Is there a predictability factor in church planting and church revitalization?" "Is it possible to predict future success?" The answer to the question is a simple "yes". Why that is true is the content of this book.

Much like the weather forecaster is able to enhance the predictability of severe storms by understanding the way the elements in the atmosphere interact to cause predictable results, the church planter and revitalization pastor must understand what components are necessary to enhance the predictability of success. Once the components have been identified, they must be assembled. The church planter and revitalization pastor are then able to enhance predictability.

I am writing this book, based on the research conducted for a doctor of ministry project, to assist church planters and church revitalization pastors in knowing and understanding the components necessary to achieve an enhanced degree of the predictability of success. Knowing the key components leading to enhanced predictability of success and how they interact will allow the leaders to know the next logical steps leading to the achievement of the vision and mission of the revitalization church or church plant. Not to know the key components leading to an enhanced predictability of success means decisions are being made in a vacuum, creating greater risk and peril. The ability to see the journey from start to finish allows for greater confidence in decision-making.

The Birth of This Project

Thirty-eight years ago, my wife and I sensed God's call for us to leave Oklahoma, where we had both been born and raised, to move to a small town in South Dakota to start a new church. We were very young. I was twenty-four, and she was nineteen. We had been married about one year.

We had never been to or even seen the place to which we were moving. We did not have a team going with us. We had one financial partner providing $300 per month. In fact, everything considered necessary today to plant a successful church was missing from our experience in starting a church. Yet, with all that was wrong with this scenario, there were many things that were right about it, which were later identified in the doctoral project undertaken thirty-eight years later.

We did not know anything about starting a church when we arrived in South Dakota in 1977. No manuals existed, no networks had been formed, and partnership had not become a part of the church planting process at that time. The term *"church planting"* did not exist.

All we were certain of was that we were called by God to be there and we were to share the gospel with as many people as possible. We did not know there were certain key components that could give us a great advantage and give us an enhanced degree of predictability that we would succeed. We obeyed God without knowing all the details, simply believing that with the call from God, the ability to carry out the vision he had given us would also come.

Thankfully, by the grace and handi-work of God, our church plant contained all the key components, discovered thirty-eight years later, that can lead to enhanced predictability of greater success. Without us even knowing what the key components consisted of, they were inherently a part of our church plant. I will forever be grateful for the grace God poured out on us as we sought to honor him.

My wife and I believed that building relationships in our new community was the most important thing we could do as we started the new church. We spent part of each day knocking on doors and meeting people. Some days people welcomed us into their homes, and some days we were not received well.

The first five months proved to be very difficult and slow. Only a few people came on Sundays to worship. Some Sundays, only Pam and I were there. But, in the dead of winter, one Sunday, forty-two people attended the service. Not one of them were people we had visited, but God was faithful and responded by bringing new people to the church. We had been faithful to share our faith, and he honored our faithfulness with great people who became the pillars of the church.

Thirty-eight years later, I would be able to prove how important relationship building is in starting a church or helping to revitalize a church. I teach in our church planting school that a church planter's first responsibility is to meet as many people as possible, as soon as possible. Nothing is more important in the building of a church than intentionally building relationships.

Over the next ten years, God did an amazing work in that small town of three thousand people. Many lives were forever changed, a solid church was established, and new churches were given birth in other towns within a sixty-mile radius of the mother church.

I have often asked these questions; "Why did our church not only survive but thrive under less than ideal circumstances when churches were not surviving all around us? Why did our church grow and develop? What was uniquely different about our church plant?"

Without knowing the key components leading to enhanced predictability of success at that time, which were highlighted in the doctoral research project conducted thirty-eight years later, I look back now and realize I understood and demonstrated those components in that first church. I apparently had internalized them in all my passion for enhanced predictability.

Thankfully, the key components of enhanced predictability of success were assembled in that church and proved to make the difference. God had called me and equipped me to bring the very keys to success to this new church. I was chosen to be blessed, and I am eternally grateful to God.

I will relate how the key components leading to enhanced predictability of success played out in this young church in the chapter identifying the key components.

The Concept of Predictability Grows

While I was serving in Phoenix, Arizona, one of the roles I fulfilled involved facilitating church planting. No framework existed to help a church plant determine the key components of success. Drawing from my past experiences, I developed a "Count the Cost" process showing the aspects of a quantitative approach.

This "Count the Cost" tool, based on Luke 14:28, "Whoever desires to build a tower, (or plant a church or revitalize a church) must first sit down and count the cost", has been very helpful over the years in showing a potential church planter, a potential partner in the work, or a revitalization pastor what the journey looks like and what needs to happen to reach each mile-marker. Understanding what needs to be done next is crucial in church planting. Church plants die many times because they react to what happens rather than be pro-active. For example, If a family is planning a road trip from Los Angeles to New York, what would they want to know to make the journey safely? Several things come to mind:

- First, which way do they drive? Driving the wrong direction in Los Angeles could mean the family could drive into the ocean and the trip would be over.
- Second, how long will it take to complete the trip? It is not possible to drive from Los Angeles to New York in a single day, so planning must include a multi-day trip complete with places to refuel, eat, and spend the night.
- Third, how much will the trip cost? Determining the financial cost of the trip is crucial to the trip being made successfully.
- Fourth, what are the mile-markers along the way to gauge progress? If Albuquerque is the first stop in the multi-day journey, be happy you have reached Albuquerque safely and not unhappy you are not in St. Louis.
- Finally, are there any bridges out along the way? If you know a bridge is out some-place on the trip, you can plan ahead and either miss it altogether or plan a safe detour.

Church planters as well as revitalization pastors must have a process much like the "Count the Cost", if they are to navigate the mine-field that is church planting and church revitalization. The Count the Cost process provides such a tool to view the journey and know what must be done to reach the desired destination. The Count the Cost process and the key components leading to an enhanced predictability of success comprise a powerful tool for the church planter.

Church Planting Is Like a Road Trip in Several Ways

- First, in planting a church or revitalizing an existing church, a sense of call and a fresh vision are vital. Starting out in the wrong direction without any understanding of the destination can result in the death of the new church or the existing church.
- Second, the ability to know how long and at what point the church can become self-sustaining provides crucial information leading to the success of the church plant or revitalization church.
- Third, the church planter or revitalization pastor must be able to know what the cost of the church plant or the existing church being revitalized will be over time. Miscalculating the cost can spell disaster for the new church. Also, not having the knowledge of the cost makes it more difficult to secure additional partners. Partners want to know how much?, how long?, and what the outcome will be if the partner is to invest?
- Fourth, the church planter or revitalization pastor must understand the stages or mile-markers the church will pass through on its journey. If a first mile-marker is set, the church planter or revitalization pastor should celebrate that he has reached this goal and not feel sad or pressured by the fact he has not yet arrived at a point for which he is not prepared. It does him no good to try to be at a place he does not have the infrastructure needed to be effective.
- Finally, for a church plant or a church in revitalization to see the journey ahead and see the point where it might run into difficulty is very important. Churches are oftentimes blind-sided by something they did not see coming, and it proves to be terminal. What if they could have seen it coming and avoided the issue altogether? That alone would enhance the predictability of success.

The Count the Cost process has served well over the years. It has given church planters, and more recently, revitalization pastors a glimpse into the future to determine if the decisions they are making today will result in success or the possibility of failure. The ability to see the future allows the church planter or revitalization pastor to make clear decisions and avoid many of the things that have caused the demise of church plants and revitalization churches that did not utilize the Count the Cost process.

The purpose of the doctoral research project was to identify the key components and join them together with the Count the Cost process, thus enhancing predictability. The data collected allowed for the design of a tool for predictability far more valuable than either process alone. Bringing the two together with the knowledge of the key components enhances the degree of predictable success in church plants and revitalization churches.

The following chapters will highlight and detail the process of identifying the key components leading to a greater enhancement of the predictability of success. The focus of the doctoral research project was to identify the key components enhancing the predictability of future success for church plants, but the principles shared in this book apply to many fields, as well as the vast revitalization arena.

Predictability is indeed all around us, if we have the ability to see it. The next pages will highlight the context of the information as it relates to church planting and revitalization and will identify the key components leading to enhanced predictability of success in both church plants and revitalized churches.

CHAPTER TWO

Church Planting Context:
My First Church Plant

My ministry of starting churches began thirty-eight years ago, before church planting was even called church planting. Partnerships were few and not very well developed at that time. Every church was like an island unto itself and the only outside financial effort was through the Cooperative Program, which was in limited supply.

The church we started in South Dakota began with just my wife and me. We received $300 per month support from a church in Arkansas. We were blessed to have a partnering church when many church planters had none. It was not a great deal of support, but it was a tremendous blessing to us.

The members of the Arkansas church took a giant leap of faith and trust to purchase an old Wesleyan Methodist Church with a capacity of seventy-five, and also provide the beginning of a salary. The people of the church prayed faithfully for us and the work. Without understanding all the details at that time, I was learning how important partnership is to the new church.

The Home Mission Board of the Southern Baptist Convention was involved in starting new churches, but to a small degree. Due to a lack of a seminary degree, I did not qualify at the time for the support the HMB offered. Little training was available for those starting the churches.

The church starters with whom I was familiar in my region had a call from God, a desire to see people saved, and an abundance of energy and perseverance. They faced many challenges but, for the most part, reacted to what was happening around them rather than be proactive. Sadly, many did not survive.

The failure rate for church plants from my vantage point in the field was extremely high. In South Dakota, over a ten-year period, I saw many churches start and many churches close their doors. In some communities, multiple attempts were made to start a church over a number of years without success.

It was tragic to watch good people struggle to start their new church only to see it fail a short time later. I often thought how different it might have been if only they had known what to do before they were on the field, as well as what to do after they started the church. I determined, if I ever had the opportunity to influence how churches were started, I would make every effort to design and develop a process to assist the church starter to be more successful.

As I recall my church planting experience in South Dakota, I thank God for his care and watch over me, my family, and our new church. South Dakota was my first full-time ministry experience. Little did I know it would be among the most difficult ministries I could have under-taken then as well as now.

The success rate for church plants in the Dakotas at that time was very low, yet our church grew and multiplied in a very small town. Why? Our church was not in a populated area. People did not come from other Baptist churches. We did not have a letter of transfer in more than nine and one-half years. It was just like all the other church plants,...or was it?

The South Dakota church experienced God's wonderful blessings but also the challenges that accompany a new work. Growth occurred, for which we were extremely grateful, but that same growth led to leadership issues. We had anticipated the issues that would arise and were able to make the necessary changes before the church "stalled" in its growth pattern.

When the church grew beyond the capacity of the original building, a new building was constructed on land given to the church by one of the original members. When the church grew beyond the capacity for teaching and training the people in small groups, the church moved to two Sunday schools. When the church filled up the space, another extension to the building was built.

Each of the situations listed above could have caused the church to slow its growth. Each situation could have been devastating to the church if the church was not prepared in advance for what was coming. Thankfully, the church was prepared for each situation faced.

Other churches did not anticipate the problems, stalled in their growth, and could not get the momentum back. They reacted to the circumstances too late. Ultimately, the churches failed.

Several aspects of the new church in South Dakota were different from other churches in the area. The key components leading to enhanced predictability of success were present, even though at the time I did not know it. Only through reflection and working with many other church plants over time did I understand what comprised the key components and that those components existed in my first church plant.

My Phoenix Church Planting Experience

A few years later I was asked to serve in Phoenix, Arizona, as the director of missions. Phoenix was a burgeoning city exploding with growth, yet the number of churches being planted proved far fewer than the number needed. Studying the history of church planting in the region, I noticed the same issues evident in South Dakota were also present in Arizona. I saw this as an opportunity I had prayed about for years to enhance the church planting process.

I asked this question: "What can be done to see successful, strong, reproducing church plants become the norm and not the exception in the Valley of the Sun?" Instinctively, I began to look at several aspects of our church in South Dakota and attempted to glean the key principles from that success and incorporate the knowledge gained into the church plants in Phoenix. What could be done to highlight the components present in the South Dakota church plant that set it apart from all the other church plants started in the region?

The context in Phoenix was totally different from South Dakota, but I felt enough commonality of the mission existed to develop a process for our churches. It was there the Count the Cost process was first utilized to allow the church planter to see the journey he was embarking upon, identify the dangers ahead, think through the issues he would face, and develop a plan to address the issues even before they happened. Count the Cost became the difference maker.

Several months after we arrived in Phoenix, a new church was started in my neighborhood by our pastor and his family and my family. The eight of us believed God was leading us to start this church. The knowledge gained in South Dakota proved to be very valuable.

The church grew dramatically from just a few meeting in a fire station to over 750 while planting sixteen other churches. Situations were anticipated and prepared for in advance. Partnership became a key to the success of the church. Relationships, which would either make the difference in success or failure, were established.

Other church plants were started in other locations deemed suitable for a strong church to develop around the Phoenix area. It was believed, with the right leader in the right place, with the right plan and the right partnership, the church would be successful. Our beliefs were correct. Many strong churches containing the key components of success discovered much later in the research project were birthed during this time.

Without knowing it, I was identifying key components leading to the enhanced predictability of success. Church plants began to grow and reproduce in a very effective way. The next ten years were filled with amazing church plants starting and growing up, making a kingdom difference. In the Phoenix context, more was learned about how the Count the Cost process transcends context, culture, geography, ethnicity, size, and style.

My Woodstock Church Planting Experience

First Baptist Church, Woodstock, (referred to as FBCW henceforth), where I currently serve, also provided a church planting context for understanding predictability. FBCW had been involved in church planting for many years and had seen a significant degree of success during that time. Even with the church's church planting success, there was still a greater desire to bring an element of predictability of success for the future. The church had made the decision to invest significant resources in multiple future church starts and, as an initial step, adopted the Count the Cost process to increase the number of successful church plants started by the church.

The Count the Cost strategy did, in fact, increase the number of church plants, but FBCW also desired a way to enhance predictability and facilitate success of future church plants. Identifying the common factors of church planting success can verify the reliability of the Count the Cost process. Through the doctoral research project, it was hoped a means of identifying the key components of enhanced predictability of church plant success would be found.

FBCW has focused its church planting efforts in areas outside the Bible belt where the evangelical witness is small. The new church must have a clear strategy to reach new people regularly or it will not survive. In these difficult areas, there is not a large number of people already serving in churches willing to transfer to the new church.

The Research Project Takes Shape

I believed a process capable of identifying key components of successful church plants would be best served through the utilization of a multi-case study. Church plants were studied in various locations over various periods. This multi-case-study approach of church plants, both within and outside the FBCW church planting system, gave a multi-faceted look at the key components of church plants from varied contexts and cultures.

The first point of concentration in the research included several practical and spiritual components in the early stages of the church planting process to identify the success factors necessary for predictability to occur. The church plants studied included church plants that started close to twenty years ago in Maricopa County, Arizona, which included Phoenix. Other church plants in the study to determine predictability included the most recent thirty-nine church plants of FBCW. Finally, church plants were selected from the eastern and western regions of the United States to give their feedback to the questions asked of the other churches.

In the Phoenix case study, the churches were started near the same time and in the same geographical region with the same opportunity for success. Each successful church planter in the study was the founding pastor and was still at his church. Each church planter answered a series of open-ended questions basically asking, in his opinion, what the key components of the success of his church plant were. Each church planter, without knowledge of any other church planter's answers, listed the same key components leading to the success of his church plant.

Church planters and people involved with the church plants starting in the same region, around the same time, with the same opportunity for success but where the church did not survive, also received the questions. Each was asked why, in their opinion, the church plant failed. Again, those involved, without the knowledge of anyone else's answer or influence, listed the same key components the successful church planters listed, only they were missing in the failed church plants.

When the common components of success were listed by both successful church plants, where the key components were present, and unsuccessful church plants, where the key components were missing, a pattern began to emerge. Utilizing the data received, a comparison was made among the thirty-nine church plants FBCW recently started. Of the thirty-nine church plants, one failed. Upon our examination, the key components of success existed in thirty-eight of the thirty-nine churches, but in one unsuccessful church plant, the key components did not exist.

The excitement generated by these findings led to further research. A successful church planter from the eastern United States and an unsuccessful church planter from the western United States received the same questions all the other church planters received. Without knowing me or anything about the study I was doing, they listed the same key components of success identified in the other case studies.

The results of the research project at this point were very exciting. Many things I had expected to find were found. However, I did not expect to find the continuity of the data that was given by the church planters.

Unexpected and Amazing Results

As I reviewed the data received from both successful and unsuccessful church plants in various locations and contexts, I concluded that enhanced predictability of church planting success is not only probable but also predictable and expected. Whenever the key components existed, church plants succeeded. The key difference proved to be having the key components in place as the church plant is starting. Subsequent chapters will identify and address the key components, but there is another application for this process pertaining to revitalization of churches in decline.

The landscape is filled with either churches not growing or churches in decline. Within the Southern Baptist Convention for example, a major focus exists whereas national and state convention staff are devoted entirely to helping churches in revitalization. Once strong and vibrant, these churches have lost people, neighborhoods have transitioned, and the leaders in the churches are now searching for something that will allow the church to be relevant again.

Analyzing the reasons for the decline of the churches, I wanted to know if a correlation existed regarding why the existing churches declined and why church plants failed. I have recently engaged several churches that were at the point of death, but, through a revitalization process I developed, I have seen a remarkable turn-around. Each revitalization church engaged in the process exhibited the same "symptoms" as the failed church plants.

The missing components of the revitalization churches proved to be the same as in the failed church plants. A conclusion can be drawn that failed church plants and declining churches have the same missing key components that lead to an enhanced predictability of success. Just as church plants that have the key components present are more likely to succeed, churches that do not have these components are more likely to continue to decline, lose effectiveness, and ultimately die.

What if the church could be infused with the key components leading to predictable success? Would that infusion make a kingdom difference? Would the church be able to turn around and become effective once again?

What Are the Key Components, and Why Are They Important?

What are the key components, and why are they so important? The following pages will outline them and illustrate why they are so important to both church plants and churches in need of revitalization. Knowing the key components becomes essential to the church plant's and revitalization church's future. It is not enough, however, to simply know the key components. These components must be assembled and utilized. To fail to intentionally seek to assemble the key components is to take the possibility of enhanced predictability away.

The list of key components on the following pages certainly is not an exhaustive list, but it does indicate what the church planters that participated in the research project identified as vitally important to the success of their church plant. The fact that all of them had commonality in identifying the key components speaks of their importance. The key components were listed in various orders throughout the process, but one key component stood out and was at the top of the list for all the people involved. The number 1 key component was leadership. The others were very important, but without leadership, nothing else mattered.

CHAPTER THREE

Key Components: Leadership

Each church plant involved in the case studies had common components listed by each one. These key components were not hinted at, coerced, or taught, but were the direct result of answers to open-ended questions. Each church planter was able to give his thoughts without any interference from any outside source.

The key components identified in this chapter and the following chapters came from both successful and unsuccessful church plants. The key components were present in the successful church plants, and the same key components were missing from the unsuccessful church plants. The discovery of this data was a very exciting part of the research and was somewhat unexpected.

Identifying the Key Components of Enhanced Predictability of Success for Church Plants and Revitalization Churches

Key Component: Leadership

The first key component providing for enhanced predictability of future success of church plants, identified as the most important was leadership. Many issues hinder the growth of church plants and revitalization churches, but based on the data discovered in the research project, having the wrong person as the leader leads to the death of church plants and revitalization churches. Regardless of the location or the presence of any other components, leadership must be present for enhanced predictability of success.

Research proved that if a church plant or revitalization church has the wrong leader, nothing else matters. Every church planter in each case study brought uniqueness, giftedness, and personality to the new church plant. However, each successful church planter possessed common key components with other successful church planters.

Leadership Involves the "It" Factor

Leadership is difficult to define, but you know it when you see it. The church planters who successfully developed their churches possessed something other church planters did not possess, ...namely, the "it" factor. The successful leaders had a presence and a quiet confidence other church planters did not possess. They were not flashy or arrogant, but each one knew who he was and what he was supposed to do, almost as an inner compass giving direction.

The Necessity and Importance of God's Call

The first common leadership trait to all successful church planters involved a clear call from God, to plant the church. The research indicated God's call meant everything and served as the steadying influence when times grew tough for the church planter and his family. God's call sustained the church planter when no other solace could and gave each church planter the opportunity to live out what God intended in his field of ministry.

Monty Patton, founding pastor of Mountain Ridge Church in Glendale, Arizona, stated, "Understanding it is God who calls people to himself, that he and he alone receives honor and glory, I therefore believe God has gifted me with the ability to draw people, love people, and engage people." Each church planter whose church plant exhibited sustained growth indicated a sense of God's call to share the gospel consistently. Patton went on to say, "One of the key components of our success rested in the fact that I am not ashamed or shy about talking to people about Jesus."

Jeremy Westbrook, founding pastor of Living Hope Church in Marysville, Ohio, stated, "After hearing of the need to plant a church, my wife and I sold all we owned and moved to Ohio because we felt called by God to do so." Dale Gross, founding pastor of Northern Hills Community Church in Phoenix, Arizona, stated, "After much prayer and a realization of a sovereign God choosing to use me, my wife and I sensed God's call to move from Indiana to Phoenix, Arizona, to start a new church.

God's call to leave the comforts of familiar surroundings and move to a place where relationships and friendships do not exist is a significant part of the enhanced predictability of the success of the church plant. Church planters who simply picked a place to go because it sounded cool or was part of someone else's strategy found they could not make the transition and completely trust God with every aspect of their future. Much like David was not able to fight with Saul's armor, the church planters lacking a clear personal call from God did not survive. The road travelled when planting a church is too rough and filled with too much danger for a person to navigate it safely apart from God's call.

Church revitalization pastors must have God's call, or the task will prove to be more difficult than they can endure. They face many challenges even church planters do not face. One factor is the past success of the church now in need of revitalization.

The past, whether great or not, will always be better in the mind of the people even when the reality indicates otherwise. My first church was a small church in the country. I remember it as a great time in a great church. The people attending felt the same way. One thing I remember clearly are the outhouses. The church did not have indoor plumbing.

Later, the church built a nice new building with indoor plumbing and nice bathrooms. They were much nicer than before, but the people kept speaking of the days of the outhouses as the greatest days of the church. I beg to disagree, but reality can never measure up to what someone holds in their memory.

God's call is a key component in enhancing the predictability of church planting success. Planting a church is not a career path choice and must be grounded in the sense of Almighty God asking you to do something special for him. God's call produced several things in the church planters who had experienced success that were missing in the church planters who did not succeed. God's call will also produce these things in pastors of revitalization churches.

God's Call Produced Things in the Church Planter's Life

First, God's call produced a genuine heart for people. The church planters knew they would likely not have the best facilities, the best equipment, or even the best ministries in town. The church planters with God's call knew, however, they had received an invitation and a mandate from God to join him in reaching people. The genuineness and authenticity of the church planters' call carried the day when nothing else would.

The prevailing thought in church planting today is that an excellent service should be provided every week. It is also thought the best equipment must be purchased and utilized to attract people. The research proved that while these things are important, nothing takes the place of having God's man, with God's call, with a genuine love for people.

God's Call Produced a Vision of the Future

God's call not only produced a heart for people but each church planter also had a clear vision of a preferred future. The church planters demonstrated an understanding of what the next steps in the journey should be. They were then able to impart that God-given vision to others. Church planters unable to formulate a preferred future into a workable and understandable vision for the people to understand did not survive.

God's Call Produced a Humble and Teachable Spirit

God's call also produced a humble and teachable spirit in the church planters who succeeded. Having a clear call from God allowed the church planters to realize that they could not accomplish the mission apart from God. Church planters exhibiting arrogance faced almost certain failure.

Arrogance proved to be the most toxic characteristic of church planters with unsuccessful church plants. By relying on their own abilities, the church planters turned their backs on God, the one true source of strength and direction, and failed. Humility and a teachable spirit marked the successful church planters' lives.

God's Call Produced a Life of Purity and Holiness

Finally, for the successful church planters, God's call produced in them a life of purity and holiness. Each one exemplified moral and ethical character laid out in God's Word. The ends never justified the means. No goal or activity to be achieved was important enough to sacrifice biblical truth. The church planters that failed, in many cases, failed in the areas of character and morality.

God's call not only produces certain things in the church planter's life and ministry but God's call also requires certain things from the church planter. It is a two-way street. God produces, but he also requires.

God's Call Requires an Understanding of Leadership Style

God's call requires several things from the church planter. God's call requires the successful church planter to have a good working understanding of his leadership style and giftedness. He must understand how to take his strengths and turn them into tools to assist in the development of other leaders. Successful church planters did so with relative ease, while church planters who failed to grow their churches were unable to develop others to share the burden of ministry. Failure to develop new leaders led to the demise of some of the church planters that participated in the research project.

God's Call Requires an Examination of Doctrine

God's call also requires an examination of doctrine, ecclesiology, and missiology. For the church planter to navigate the minefield of church planting a clear understanding of doctrine is required. Many opinions were gathered from the church planters in the study, but the ones with a solid biblical grounding about who they were and what they believed managed to stay focused and on track with their vision.

Other church planters in the study, who were unsure of their doctrinal belief found people could sway them in a different direction. They allowed someone to hijack their vision. The people hijacking the vision were not mean but, in many cases, were good people who wanted to do good things. The problem is that what they did drew the pastor, and ultimately, the church away from its primary mission.

They lost focus and ultimately lost momentum, and the church plant died. The church planters who started with the mentality to reach neighbors and nations from the beginning proved to have greater success than the church planters who were more concerned about their situation. Focus is critically important.

God's Call Requires the Church Planter to Develop His Skills

God's call requires the church planter to know and develop his giftedness and skill-set. The church planters in the study did not have the same personality or the same gift or skill-set. Each brought his own uniqueness to the ministry field.

The church planters who excelled enhanced their giftedness and constantly improved on the skills God had given them. The church planters in the studies, who, for whatever reason, believed they already had what it takes to successfully plant a church soon realized they did not have all the answers. By then it was too late.

God's Call Requires an Evaluation of Strategic Capabilities

God's call also requires an evaluation of the church planter's strategic capabilities such as vision, entrepreneurship, leadership, and execution. The successful church planters did not take their capabilities for granted. They always evaluated all aspects of what their call entailed and sought to clarify and improve on every area.

Church planters that participated in the research project who did not survive could not articulate and convey a clear vision. They did not execute well and tried to do everything without the help of others. Entrepreneurs know they need more than what they have, and they engage others to join them in moving forward together. Those who sought to raise money to *buy* leadership rather than develop indigenous leaders did not survive. It is always easier to raise money than to develop leaders.

The Importance of God's Call Cannot Be Overestimated

The importance of the call of God in a church planter's life cannot be overstated. Without it, the church planter will struggle. When loneliness sets in, the church planter will have a hard time staying in a difficult situation without the assurance that comes from a divine call. No other ingredient carries the strength of the call of God for a church planter than the certainty he is where he is supposed to be, doing what he is supposed to do for such a time as this.

Vision Is Also a Key Component of the Leader

Another key component of the leader of successful church plants is the ability of the leader to develop and articulate a clear vision and ministry plan to share with the people in the new church. From the research, the successful church planters were able to draw a clear future picture of the church showing what could be if the people would follow after God. Unsuccessful church planters could not articulate a clear and compelling vision people could understand.

Simply stated, a future picture is a view of the future as we would like it to be. To establish a new church that is healthy, the future picture is a must. Basically, three things must happen if a new church is to succeed:

1. People must be reached with the gospel. Jesus tells the disciples, power will come when the Holy Spirit will come, and they shall be witnesses in Jerusalem, Judea, Samaria, and the uttermost parts of the earth (Acts 1:8). Jesus's Great Commission in Matthew 28:19–20 leaves no doubt about the role of evangelism.

    Robby Gallaty stated, "The word *"go"* in the Great Commission is the missionary aspect. Every believer is to participate in taking the gospel to others. The word *"baptize"* is the relational aspect. The word *"teach"* is the rational aspect."

Church plants with an intentional and aggressive plan to present the gospel grew into strong and healthy churches.

2. People must be made into disciples. Matthew 28 focuses on the idea of disciple-making by using the words *"make disciples"* as the key action of the words. The idea of making disciples involves sharing the teachings of Jesus with others who will in turn share it with others. Gallaty provides insight into the process with a four-step progression Jesus initiated with his disciples:

    •   First, Jesus ministered while the disciples watched. In the Sermon on the Mount, Jesus taught God's truths, and the disciples observed, listened, and learned.
    •   Second, Jesus progressed to allowing the disciples to assist him in ministry. When feeding the multitude, Jesus broke the bread and performed the miracle. The disciples distributed the bread and collected the surplus.
    •   Third, the disciples ministered, and Jesus assisted them. In Mark 9, the disciples attempted to cast out a demon but could not. Jesus stepped in and cast out the demon.
    •   Fourth, Jesus observed as the disciples ministered to others. Jesus sent them out with power into the world.

    Rick Warren stated, "This strategy of starting churches brings into question the reason for the existence of the church. Evangelism as the means of reaching people with the gospel forms an important part of the answer regarding why the church exists." The answer to the question why the church exists sets up the reason for evangelism leading to consideration of church planting.

    Stuart Murray declared, "Early disciples were to go, make disciples, baptize, and teach. The only way for this mandate to be carried out until Christ's second coming was through communities of believers in particular geographical areas." The early stages of the church involved small groups of people with similar backgrounds and needs covenanting together to care for one another and to fulfill God's mandate and mission.

The establishment of small communities of believers provided the framework through which the mission and mandate of God could come to pass. J. D. Payne stated, "The Apostolic Church was given the mandate to bear witness to Christ and his resurrection by making disciples of all nations." The successful church plants in the research project took seriously the command of Jesus to share the good news.

Jesus's commission to his followers to intentionally reach out to all of God's creation through evangelism and disciple-making led to the church's growth. The church plants in the research project that were intentional about sharing the gospel and making disciples grew and flourished, while the church plants holding the idea that people would automatically come and be committed followers of Jesus did not survive.

3. People must be deployed in ministry. A new church must be able to present to new believers clearly defined ways for them to be involved in service to the Lord and his church. The new churches seriously committed to reaching people, making disciples of people, and deploying people in ministry with clearly defined roles saw the ministry of the church expand as people were placed in service.

No church can grow beyond its leadership capacity. Leaders must constantly be developed. Church plants not developing leaders and trusting them to serve soon found the church planter overwhelmed, burnt out, and soon gone from the church plant, which, in turn, died soon after.

Each successful church planter understood the importance of reaching people, making disciples, and deploying people in ministry. What they understood beyond that was the need for a clear and compelling vision to illustrate for the people in the church the plan as to how the three very important objectives would be achieved. The church planter's ability to paint that future picture in high-resolution living color was key to the church plant's success.

Patton stated, "The development of a vision or strategy plan, as we call it, helped me plan for future growth, leadership development, stewardship, and evangelism. I also knew from the plan the amount of resources available for staff, facilities, mission, and ministry." Westbrook stated, "It is not unbiblical to put together a strategy enabling the church plant to move from point 'A' to point 'B', and do it well."

In every instance there was the overpowering sense that the successful church planters had the ability to visualize what God asked them to do. They also had the ability to share it in such a way that others saw it, understood it, and helped carry it out. Will Browning, founding pastor of Journey Church, Summerville, North Carolina, stated, "We spent years developing our vision and carefully chose the language to transmit the vision to our people. The vision brought clear expectations and created fuels and filters that would guide us forward."

Vision was not something that just happened. Vision was sought, developed, and shared. The church planters who were unsuccessful either did not have a vision or did not possess the ability to share it in a way that the people could understand. Let me illustrate this point:

Imagine we are best friends and we are at our favorite baseball game. I tell you I will buy the hotdogs if you will go get them. With the information I gave you, what are the chances you will get the hotdog I really want? The answer is not a very good chance. There is not enough solid information to go on and thousands of possibilities.

Now, consider this scenario. I will buy the hotdogs if you will go pick them up. I want the half-pounder, not some skinny hotdog. I want it with mustard, relish, and chili on a plate with two napkins. Now, what are the odds? The odds are much better than before. The stated outcome is backed up by clear, high-resolution details, making the next step obvious.

Vision Is Helping People Know What Kind of Hotdog You Want

Vision proved to be a key component in successful church plants. The ability to have enough information allows the person to visualize what kind of hotdog you really want and provide it for you. The successful church planters were able to share a clear enough vision that the people knew what kind of hotdog was expected. Armed with that knowledge, they were able to execute well.

Love for People A Key Component of Successful Pastors

Successful church planters demonstrated a love for people. Mark Lashey, founding pastor of Lifehouse Church, Middletown, Delaware, stated, "The Lord gave me a specific intense burden and love for our community, but more importantly for the people living in the community." Each church planter committed unreservedly to minister the love of God to people entrusted to the ministry of each new church.

The successful church planter's greatest concerns did not consist of physical trappings or personal agendas. The greatest concerns focused upon building and strengthening relationships. Gross stated, "The church planter must enter into this calling with a 'whatever-it-takes attitude' to fulfill God's mission in the community." Humility and teach-ability defined each successful church planter.

The successful church planters did not feel all-knowing, but did possess a desire to learn from others. Jim Collins stated, "The best and most successful leader constantly asks, "Why?" He or she continually learns without arrogance." Each successful church planter knew God's vision and pursued that vision with a high degree of integrity. No substitute existed for pure leadership.

Throughout the research, we found the difference in the leader of the successful church plants and the leader of the unsuccessful church plants was like night and day. The difference was evident in attitude, outlook, execution, and the ability to draw others into the vision. It is of little wonder why leadership was the one ingredient that must be present for success to follow. Without leadership, once again, nothing else matters.

So, without a leader with a call, a vision, and a love for people, the church plant is destined to fail. Along with leadership other key components are necessary to enhance predictability of success. The second key component enhancing the predictability factor for church plants is the place the church is planted.

The Place the Church Is Planted Is a Key Component

All locations are possible, but some places are optimal. The location of a successful church plant contains so many variables detailing each variable would prove impossible. In selecting the place to plant a church, successful church planters identified many possible locations, but realized all locations did not prove to be ideal. Patton stated, "Two strong churches negotiated for five acres in a prime location prior to my arrival. Having a future secured was a key component to our success."

The "identity of place" is so strong in some locations that to fail to secure "a place" means the church plant loses all credibility with the population. The research indicated the capability to provide a place had a great deal to do with the success of the church plant. Gross stated, "In one of the churches our church sponsored, the wife had come from a large church with many ministries. After a few months, she determined she could not live without all the amenities of a large church. The church plant was doomed."

The successful church planters surveyed and involved in the research spent much time and went to great lengths to understand the spiritual potential of the place for the new church. Determining if the place the church planter desired to plant the church would be the best place could not be random or taken lightly. Selection of place must be done with much prayer and forethought.

One of my roles as minister of church planting is simply to seek out potential places where a new church could be started with a high degree of confidence of success. The places sought are places where others have chosen not to go. They are places where potential partners are likely already on the ground. They are places where it is evident God has already been there before us.

The church planters in the churches that did not succeed paid little attention to the location of the new church. Some selected a place out of convenience, meaning, they were willing to start a church as long as it was within a few miles of where they grew up. Others listened to some other person or some other entity and "chose" a place for its cool factor. And still others simply did not realize the critical importance of the location.

Issues to Consider

The following represents the most-mentioned issues each church and church planter must consider:

- First, the area the church plant is to be started must fit within the mission strategy of the partnering or sending church.
- Second, the area must contain a community under-served by evangelical churches.
- Third, the area can be reached more effectively if the sending church has previous experience in the region.
- Fourth, the context of the church plant area must match the church planter.

The results of the research project indicated the person and the place cannot be overestimated in the potential for success. The wrong person may undermine the entire church plant. The wrong person in the wrong place compounds the issue. The wrong person in the wrong place at the wrong time makes it almost impossible to succeed. Along with the person and the place, partnership is identified by successful church planters as one of the key components of success.

Partnership Identified as a Key Component

Partnership brought several important aspects to the church plants:

- Clearly defined expectations: Issues arose that could have hindered the new church if the role and expectations of all partners had not been clearly articulated and understood. Covenants between partners allowed for all parties to provide best practice at all times.
- Accountability: Perhaps the most important role for any partnership involved providing accountability for the church planter and the church planting team. Accountability for how the church plants progressed, problems the church planters encountered, and how the partnership assisted the church planters provided the church planters a sense of strength and continuity.
- Involvement of other churches: Each partner provided prayer covers, resources, and man-power, which allowed the church plant to accomplish things not possible alone.

Partnering with another church, multiple churches, or national entities surfaced in the research as a key component common to successful church plants. Patton stated, "The partnership met with me once each month for over two years, giving me counsel, insight, encouragement, and help with direction. I am not sure Mountain Ridge Church would have survived without partnership."

Lashey stated, "A strong support system from convention entities and churches like First Baptist Church, Woodstock, and the Woodstock Church Planting School have been a critical component to our success." The FBCW Church Planting School demonstrates how partnering churches can be of assistance to new church plants.

Partnership for the purpose of securing resources, accountability, coaching, and mentoring proved to be a vital key component for the church planters. Each partnership was designed differently, but the church planters recognized the importance of partnership for their church plant. The partnership infused energy and gave a point of accountability for the church planters.

Developing a Plan Identified as a Key Component

The next key component needed to enhance the predictability of success was a plan. The successful church planters in the research project had a concise plan of action to achieve clear and achievable objectives. Vision carried the idea of a preferred future, and the plan helped the church planters achieve the stated vision.

Each church planter felt he had been provided a way to "see" into the future and observe the whole journey. By doing so, the church planter anticipated problems, dealt with the problems effectively, or avoided the problems altogether. Each aspect of the church planting process gave the church planter and partners in the church plant a way to fulfill agreed-upon outcomes for the church plant.

Westbrook stated, "It is critically important to count the cost in ministry. I have watched many church planters with a call from God and great church connections fail because they do not count the cost." Gross stated "The church planter and his partners in ministry must be faithful to follow God's plan." Church planters not utilizing the Count the Cost process oftentimes did not have a clear understanding of the amount of support needed, and, as a result, received inadequate support, and ultimately, the church plant died.

Grace Church, in Albuquerque, New Mexico, the one church plant from First Baptist Church, Woodstock that did not survive over the past five years, provided a clear example of the need for partnership. Grace Church and the church planter indicated additional partnership through additional churches and individuals as forthcoming; however, when the additional support did not materialize, Grace Church did not survive. Partnership commitments must be secured before the new church is started.

Leadership Development Identified as A Key Component

The successful church planters also possessed an ability to reproduce themselves, thus allowing more people to share in the fulfillment of the vision. Patton stated, "A God-called leader will make or break a church plant." Westbrook stated, "When God calls leaders, he expects them to lead." Browning stated, "Church planters often have an idea but cannot transmit that into something others will accept and follow." Lashey stated, "God has provided a diverse yet unified team of people willing to do whatever it takes."

Leadership, or the lack of leadership, played a key role in each of the churches in the case studies. The successful church plants recognized the need for leadership, while the unsuccessful church plants lacked a person who could lead. Leadership and leader development proved, based on the research, to be the number 1 key component for predictability of future church plant success.

Realistic Expectations Identified as a Key Component

Realistic expectations proved vitally important to the church planters identified in the research. The successful church planters did not allow unrealistic expectations to dominate the church plant. Damage caused by unrealistic expectations can and often did prove irreparable. The successful church planters managed expectations well and used those managed expectations to an advantage.

Ed Stetzer highlighted realistic expectations in a report to the North American Mission Board in 2004. Stetzer stated, "A church plant's viability could increase as much as 250 percent as a result of realistic expectations." Without realistic expectations, any strategy faces serious issues. Inflated and unachievable expectations provided no benefit to the church planters in the research for this project. In fact, unrealistic expectations may have contributed to the downfall of many.

Successful church planters identified leadership, and in particular, leadership of the church planter, as the number 1 key component. The successful church planters surveyed also included in the list of key components the place, partnership, plan, vision, leadership development, and realistic expectations. The key components leading to enhanced predictability of success were clearly visible.

Unsuccessful church plants in the research provided key data as well. Data for this category came from a state convention person who worked directly with church planters, colleagues, partners, other church planters, and from First Baptist Church, Woodstock's, church planting ministry records. This research proved to be very valuable since understanding why something does not work is necessary to this project's validity.

Compilation of the data indicated the number 1 key component missing from unsuccessful church plants mirrored the number 1 key component of leadership of the church planter identified in successful church plants. The unsuccessful church plants identified a lack of leadership as the key reason the churches did not survive. Failure to invest in the development of other potential leaders added to the demise of the church.

Lashey stated, "I am sure one of the reasons church plants in my region did not survive and did not experience success involved a lack of commitment and a willingness to sacrifice." Patton added, "Another reason church plants in my region did not survive related to the fact the church planter tried to "pastor" the people too quickly. The church planter settled down with fifty to seventy-five people and ceased to function as a missionary." In church planting, leadership, or the lack of leadership, must always face scrutiny. The research indicated church plants with a strong leader had a much greater predictability of success than those without a strong leader.

Church plants that failed to survive also held in common the lack of a clearly defined vision for the church and its future. Browning stated, "If a church planter cannot cast vision in a compelling way where outsiders get excited, he will not succeed." The role of the church planter rested in the ability to paint a picture for people, allowing each person to *own* the vision in a tangible way.

Vision allowed people to see the role each person played in moving the church plant toward a common goal. Unsuccessful church plants did not provide a picture of the preferred future like the successful church plants provided. Successful church planters understood the importance and value of vision.

A lack of a definite plan of action surfaced in the research for this project as a common thread in the unsuccessful church plants. Unsuccessful church plants did not follow a plan of outreach or leadership development. Successful church plants made much of a personal desire to see more people come into the kingdom and be prepared for face-to-face encounters.

Patton stated, "The reasons why some church plants failed, even when given the same opportunities, can be attributed to their inability or unwillingness to engage people personally. Get out of Starbucks and get off the computer, and tell someone about Jesus!" Dennis Adams, founding pastor of The Church @ Arrowhead, stated, "Making disciples who follow Jesus must be the church's first priority . . . first things first." Gross stated, "The new church must build relationships and community from the beginning to be successful."

Research showed a dramatic difference in church plants with a Count the Cost church planting process in place and those that did not have access to the Count the Cost process. The Count the Cost church planting process indicated the amount of partnership needed and the length of time the partnership members committed support. Patton stated, "I have watched some church plants fail because they either did not have a plan or they did not follow the plan in place. They did not do the necessary things to reach new people, got out of balance with finances, or did not develop enough leaders." Lashey added, "We do not simply ask people to join us, we intentionally ask our people to engage and reach out to the residents of our city."

The Count the Cost Process Made a Distinct Difference

The Count the Cost process made a distinct difference in the church plants that participated in the research. The research also focused on successful church plants not engaged previously in a Count the Cost church planting process. As we realized many church plants grow to be strong, healthy, and reproducing churches without the Count the Cost process, it was important to note for this research what difference could be determined for those churches using the Count the Cost process.

A comparison indicated the successful church plants that utilized the Count the Cost process and the successful church plants that did not utilize the Count the Cost process, held the same key components in common. Will Browning, a successful church planter who did not utilize the Count the Cost process, listed the key components leading to success as, "Leadership, including a clear call from God, clearly articulated vision, partnership, leader development, and reproducible systems."

The results of the research served as a confirmation that when certain key components existed at the start of the church plant, the enhanced predictability of success existed as well. The final category of research explored unsuccessful church plants utilizing the Count the Cost church planting process. Following the pattern of the previous research, we found that unsuccessful church plants that utilized the Count the Cost process also exhibited some of the same key components as successful church plants had at the beginning of the journey.

Over the first few months, however, the church plants failed to keep the emphasis on the key components and moved toward a less accountable situation and did not hold the key components as priorities. Unsuccessful church plants had a great opportunity of success, since some of the key components existed, but these churches did not take advantage of specific opportunities and focused on things unimportant to the growth and development of the church plant.

Difference Noted Between Church Plants That Utilized the Count the Cost Process and Church Plants That Did Not Utilize the Count the Cost Process

One difference did surface, however. The number of church plant failures happened at a much greater rate in the church plants that did not utilize the Count the Cost process than the unsuccessful church plants that utilized the Count the Cost church planting process. Stetzer stated, "The failure rate of church plants is reaching nearly 40 to 50 percent nationally." The failure rate of church plants utilizing the Count the Cost church planting process currently stands at 4 percent over the past five years of church planting through First Baptist Church, Woodstock.

Research also revealed lack of partnership as a common denominator of unsuccessful church plants. Grace Church, a failed church plant from First Baptist Church, Woodstock, started with the belief people and churches making a verbal commitment to the church plant would follow through with those commitments. The anticipated financial support from the partnership did not materialize although the church had already started. Starting before having all commitments signed proved to be fatal for Grace Church.

The premise of the project that an enhanced degree of predictability for future church plant success exists in church plants exhibiting certain key components proved accurate. The successful church plants clearly identified the key components and utilized each one to grow and strengthen the church plant. The churches that did not survive identified the lack of the key components.

As you might also expect from the research, the degree of success was in direct proportion to the degree the key components were identified and utilized. Several of the successful churches grew with great speed and without much difficulty. Others grew at a more modest rate, but each one was able, over time, to recognize the key components and incorporate them into their new church. Failure to take note of the key components and to utilize them proved fatal to some of the churches in the research project.

CHAPTER FOUR

Expectations Identified and Evaluated

In virtually every situation that each of us faces, there are feelings, emotions, and expectations. This exercise was filled with pre-conceived ideas, thoughts, and attitudes that could have had a dramatic effect on the outcome. For that reason, the research was conducted in such a way that the results could be as pure as possible without being overly tainted by previous ideas.

Without question, considering my past and my fascination with predictability, I had several pre-conceived ideas:

- First, I was convinced in my mind that enhanced predictability existed in the world. I had seen it play out for years and knew, when circumstances were right, certain reactions occurred with great predictability. At least this phenomenon was true in the physical realm. Whether it held true in the human-driven realm was still to be determined.
- Second, I believed that if a predictability factor did exist, it could revolutionize the way churches are planted and increase the success rate tremendously. It could also provide a solid process for potential partners to connect with and strengthen the new church. I do not discount prayer or the fact that God can do whatever he pleases, but in scripture the person God

desires to use has several things he must do to make ready for what God does.

On the mountain when God's prophet challenged the prophets of Baal, we find it to be true that God has conditions. Baal's prophets attempted to call down fire to consume the sacrifice to no avail. All day long they persisted, but their god did not show up. Regardless of their efforts, no response came from their god.

Then God's prophet took the stage. Before he started to call down fire from heaven, he was instructed by God with several things to do. He was informed he was to repair the altar, dig the ditches, and pour water on the sacrifice. Once he had done what God instructed and fulfilled God's criteria, he knelt down and called on God to let the fire fall, and he did.

Scripture is filled with "If...Then" passages. One such passage of note is found in 2 Chronicles 7:14, "If my people, which are called by my name, shall humble themselves, and pray, and seek my face, and turn from their wicked ways; then will I hear from heaven, and will forgive their sin, and heal their land."

God speaks often with if...then statements. He says something will occur if other things are done. He has conditions, and when his conditions are met, he responds accordingly.

Once God has conditions, then it becomes even more important to know what those conditions are so they can be met. The research for *The Predictability Factor* was an attempt to discover the conditions, or key components, through which enhanced predictability could exist. Once discovered, enhanced predictability could be expected.

• Third, not only did I believe in my heart predictability existed in the world and a predictability factor could revolutionize church planting, I also believed certain criteria must be met to see predictability realized. So, what key components make up the conditions through which predictability operates?

Inherently, before any research occurred, I believed leadership to be the most critical component. I had seen churches and church plants struggle due to a lack of leadership. Leadership is difficult to define, but you know it when you see it.

As I contemplate today, after the research has concluded and proven certain things to be true, I desire to incorporate the key components of enhanced predictability into my church plants. In all of First Baptist Church, Woodstock's, church plants started in under-served and difficult areas over the past few years, only one of thirty-nine did not survive. I asked the question "why" and began to study it.

As my study progressed, I found that the one that failed to survive did not contain the key components of enhanced predictability. All the other church plants that were thriving contained the key components. In the one failed church plant, it turned out we had the wrong person in the wrong place at the wrong time. The lack of partnership and vision surfaced as the missing key components. Leadership was at the core of this failure.

Expectations Completely Blown Away

As the project began, I expected to receive answers from the church planters and glean a nugget of information from each one that might lead to a consensus of ideas around which I could build an argument for enhanced predictability. Nothing could have prepared me for what occurred. Never would I have expected the results found in the research project.

As the first information began to be received, the church planter was focused on the questions and was very clear and concise with his answers. It was as if he had the questions in his possession for a long time and developed a well-thought-out answer. However, the church planters were asked the questions without any indication of what they would be before-hand.

With each question, the church planter seemed so confident in his answers and articulated clearly and concisely what he perceived to be the key components of his success. No hesitation and no uncertainty. This appeared to be something that went deep into his heart and not some surface issue. Calmly and surely, he shared what the key components were and why each was important.

Honestly, I was not prepared for what I received. I had expected an incomplete answer at best. I thought I would only get a part of the picture, not what I received. I thought perhaps this was an anomaly and the other data would be more of what I had expected.

I entered into the second church planter's response unsure of what to expect. As I began to examine the answers to the questions, once again I sensed confidence in the way the church planter presented the data. He was confident but not arrogant. He knew what he was talking about and had committed it to his heart. What he was telling me was not like reading a script but rather like sharing an important and impactful season in his life.

The church planter's answers were filled with passion and made me feel as if I were living it with him. The events were like fresh paintings with great detail and high resolution. I had expected fragments and partial answers, but these were complete.

The second church planter shared the key components that led to his success. When the data was analyzed, the components listed matched perfectly to those of the first church planter. Was it coincidence? Was it blind luck? What were the odds?

By this time I was finding the answers to the questions very intriguing. I could not wait to get to the next church planter. What would I discover there?

As the answers to the third set of questions began to be analyzed, I sensed a quiet confidence on the part of the church planter once again. By this time I was expecting clarity and certainty. I was not disappointed. The answers to the third set of questions ended with the church planter listing the same key components as the other church planters had done. I felt at this point I was on to something very important and very special.

In each of the questionnaires and times of interaction with successful church planters, there was a quiet calmness and an ability to share what was in their heart with clarity. In answers to each set of questions, the church planters indicated the same key components that existed in their church plant. I was overwhelmed by what I received from them.

If successful church plants contained the same key components, then what contributed to the lack of success of other church plants? I went back to the region where the successful church plants had been birthed and sought out people who had been part of an unsuccessful church plant, as well as people who knew of the work. The failed church plants had been started in the same region, at the same time, and with the same opportunity to succeed, but had failed to do so. Why?

As I began the research on the failed church plants, it was quickly evident that this event in their lives had left an indelible mark they would carry for a very long time. There seemed to be a great sense of sadness yet with clarity of thought. The information gathered from the first failed church listed the reasons why the church failed. The same list of key components listed by the successful church planters emerged as missing in the failed church.

Wow! I did not expect to discover what I discovered. I thought it would be something totally different. Yet, the key components listed were exactly the same as the successful churches but were listed as missing components in the failed churches. Again, I thought, *Could this be coincidence? Could it simply be luck?*

As I continued to learn from the failed church plants, ultimately the same components were identified as missing. I started to think there must be something to this beyond what I saw on the surface. Could it be the key components are universal and if they are present the church has an enhanced predictability of success? If so, the data would have a wide range of applications.

I imagined what this could mean to the church planting community as a whole but was not yet ready to make the claim that enhanced predictability is not only possible but expected. I examined the church plants of First Baptist Church, Woodstock, and found that the successful church plants had the key components and the one that failed lacked the key components.

Evaluating Expectations

Based on my experience with weather predictions, I expected to find a correlation between the key components and successful church plants. It was not a great surprise to find such a correlation existed. It was also not a surprise that the key components could be identified.

What proved to be very surprising was the fact that the key components identified were present to some degree in every successful church plant and missing to some degree in unsuccessful church plants. Also surprising was the degree of certainty each planter held regarding the key components. Each component stood out in their mind very vividly, allowing them to share it with great clarity and passion, as though they were just now living it, yet for most of the church planters, it had been many years since they had started their new church.

Revitalization Churches and the Data

I wondered if the key components might be missing in churches in need of revitalization. My wondering remained just that until I began working with several revitalization churches on a close, personal level.

What I discovered helped me understand my wonderment was indeed fact.

Each church in need of revitalization was missing, to some degree, all or part of the key components discovered in the research project. Having the ability to know what to look for made the process of helping the churches much more simple. I knew for the church to turn around and be effective once again, the key components must be assembled.

One by one, as the churches dealt with finding and implementing the key components into their church, the church began to come to life. It was possible to literally see the light of hope come back into their eyes. The more the key components grafted into the revitalization church, the stronger it became. As in the cases of successful church plants having the key components, the revitalization churches that incorporated the key components into the life of the church became successful once more.

CHAPTER FIVE

Lessons Learned From the Research Project

Several lessons were learned through conducting this research project. The lessons learned were varied. Some lessons were personal, and some ministry based. All lessons learned proved very valuable moving forward.

Personally, I researched church history to try to discover a tool that had been used to predict future success of new churches, but I found none. I thought perhaps in all the stages of history, somewhere there would be a pattern of success leading to a common instigator, but I found none. I thought, surely, with all the scholars and movements through the ages, something existed to help predict success, but nothing stood out.

I discovered that the closest thing to a tool to predict future success was a process I developed years ago called, "Count the Cost," based on Luke 14:28, "If anyone among you desires to build a tower, (plant a church), let him first sit down and count the cost." The Count the Cost process indicates to the church planter where the church currently stands and, reasonably, where it might be in the future. It also indicates what it will take for the church to reach each specific mile-marker on its journey.

Successful church planters seemed to have an inner sense about what needed to be done to move the church forward. The Count the

Cost process lays out for them what to expect if certain things are put in place. With a great degree of accuracy, the church planter can visualize what the decisions he is making today will look like tomorrow.

The ability to literally look into the future means the church planter has a tremendous edge on those who do not have access to the Count the Cost. The church planter sees the high points, but equally important, he is able to see the dangers far in advance and make appropriate adjustments to avoid difficult situations. Nothing catches the church planter by surprise if he has the Count the Cost process in place.

The Count the Cost process gives the church planter valuable insight, utilizing the assumptions he has made regarding his church plant. For example: the church planter determines a reasonable growth pattern based on what he knows and is able to learn about the area. Count the Cost then tabulates for him such things as when, and how many new small groups must be in place. In direct correlation, Count the Cost provides the number and the date when additional leaders are needed to avoid a loss of momentum.

Loss of momentum in a church plant is a recipe for disaster. Failure to provide adequate space may lead to a loss of momentum. Lack of leaders when needed also contributes to a loss of momentum. The Count the Cost process allows the church planter to be prepared at all times.

Also available to the church planter with the Count the Cost process is the ability to determine the degree of partnership support needed and how long it will be needed. This aspect also gives the church planter a tremendous advantage when talking to potential partners. The church planter has the knowledge of what is needed and the capability to show a potential partner.

The potential partner wants to know three basic things when the church planter seeks out his support:

- The first thing a potential partner wants to know is, "*how much?*" He does not want a ballpark figure or even a good guess.

The potential partner wants an accurate and realistic amount. He also does not want to be the only partner. If a church planter has only one partner, the new church is at risk. If something would happen to the pastor of the partner church or there would be a conflict, the new church plant could lose its support and ultimately die. It is infinitely better for a new church to have multiple partners not only for financial reasons but also for prayer and manpower.

- The second thing a potential partner wants to know from the church planter is, *"How long?"* He wants to know how long you need his support. He wants to know at what point you fore-see the church plant able to stand on its own. No potential partner wants to get involved with an open-ended commitment. There must be a clear sunset indicated.

- The third thing a potential partner desires to know is, *"What outcome can be expected?"* The potential partner investing in the church plant wants to know his investment is going to produce results. The Count the Cost process answers each of the questions potential partners ask.

Benefits of Counting the Cost: Never Caught Off Guard

Count the Cost allows the new church planter to never get caught off guard or unprepared. Several scenarios highlight the points at which the church planter can be caught off guard. For example: imagine the new church has a capacity of 90 people, but in the growth pattern of the church plant by the end of the second year, the attendance is projected to be 110. The new church will never reach 110 with 90 seats unless something is done to provide more capacity.

The new church planter would need to understand that in less than two years, the church would need to function in a different way to reach 110. The new church would need to secure another facility, which may not be available, or, if available, not affordable, or move to multiple services, requiring additional leaders that must be trained. Failure to notice this problem waiting ahead or failure to prepare early enough in advance could cause the new church to lose momentum.

One of the most difficult things to maintain in a church plant moving forward is positive momentum. Several of the church plants that did not succeed always found the church playing "catch-up" after dealing with a crisis. After so many stalls, the new church did not have the energy to move ahead. Successful church plants utilizing the Count the Cost process could anticipate crises and make adjustments far enough in advance to minimize the issue and keep momentum.

Another example highlighting a point at which a church planter might be caught off-guard is in the area of leadership. Leadership is the single thread tying everything else together throughout the research process. I have not discovered a church that can say it has more leaders than it needs. Generally, the opposite is true, and the church is in need of leaders.

Unless the church planter pays attention to his situation very carefully, he can wake up one day and realize he is doing everything. Failure to intentionally focus on leader development led to the deaths of several churches. Throughout scripture, the theme of leadership is woven into the fabric of the text. Moses was under great pressure to make decisions, and the burden was too heavy to bear.

Moses sought advice and was told what he was doing was not good. He needed other leaders to assist him and share the burden with him. Church planters must spend a large portion of their time in two areas, the first is reaching people, and the second is developing leaders.

The successful church planters in the research project had the ability to develop other leaders. They also had the trust level to allow each one to assume responsibility within the new church plant. Count the Cost lets them see how many leaders were needed and when.

Patton stated, "A God-called leader will make or break a church plant." Westbrook shared, "When God calls leaders, he expects them to lead." Browning added, "Church planters often have an idea but cannot transmit that into something others will accept and follow." Lashey stated, "God has provided a diverse yet unified team of people willing to do whatever it takes."

Leadership, or the lack of leadership, played a key role in each of the churches in the case studies. The successful church plant recognized the need for leadership, while the unsuccessful church plants lacked a person who could lead. The importance of leadership development cannot be overstated. Leadership was the difference between life and death.

Personally, I had searched for a tool to aid in predicting future success of church plants but did not find one. Count the Cost, however, provided the necessary framework for the research to flow and give indication of the potential for success. Count the Cost provided the quantitative aspect, while the key components related to the qualitative aspect of the research.

Lesson Learned: Enhanced Predictability Is Possible

Enhanced Predictability is possible. That is a very powerful statement. That statement removes all excuses and brings accountability into play. Accountability is needed on the part of the church planter to make sure he has done the things needed to enhance the predictability of success. The sending church and other partners must now make sure the key components are in play before the new church starts.

Lesson Learned: Enhanced Predictability Changes the Game

I learned enhanced predictability changes the game. The rules, as well as the outcome are now different. No longer can a church planter fail to secure the key components and claim some other reason for the failure of the new church. Enough examples surfaced in the research to prove certain things coming together have a predictable outcome. Church planters not recognizing the correlation between the key components and predictable outcomes are inviting failure into their situation.

Successful church plants, and by *successful* I mean the church plant fulfilled the purpose for which it was started, have been those in which the church planters inherently knew what it took to achieve their mission. No secret formula exists. No certain type of person is needed. It is not as simple as that, but it is not as complicated as some want to make it.

In the research, there were many different church planters with different skill sets, different personalities, and different temperaments. The person was vitally important, but not a particular type of person. The key to success involved a leader and the key components coming together and reacting.

When I planted my first church many years ago, it was thought at that time only someone with an extrovert personality could successfully plant a church. As it turns out, I am an introvert and do not possess the qualities deemed necessary to plant a church in my day, yet, not only did we plant our church, but we also planted churches around us in a radius of sixty miles.

If the key components are present and the church is successful with an extrovert or an introvert, the game has certainly been changed. I have long believed an average leader placed in a great system will excel. By the same logic, a great leader placed in a bad system will struggle. The research seems to have borne out the fact that leadership is critical, but the system is also an important piece of the puzzle.

Lesson Learned: The Predictability Factor Affects Existing Churches Too

The research project started out as a way to identify the key components to be able to enhance the predictability of future success of church plants. It was not long before the knowledge gained could be applied to existing churches, especially churches in need of revitalization. This opened up another exciting vein of discovery.

I have worked with many churches in revitalization consultations, and the parallel became very pronounced. The churches in need of revitalization placed alongside the church plants that did not survive were striking in their similarities. The key components of the successful church plants were, to some degree, missing in the revitalization churches.

In one church, it might be a lack of leadership or a lack of vision. Some churches in need of revitalization had a person leading them without a clear call from God to lead the church forward. Still others there was no plan or clear knowledge of what the people in the community needed. In almost every case, the churches were out of balance. By that I mean the church spent its resources on staff or buildings and had long since ceased funding ministries or missions.

What do these churches need? They need an understanding of where they are and how they came to be in this situation. Once they know why they are there, the church needs to begin to think and act as if it were a church plant. The church needs to secure leadership, re-engage the community, develop an outreach and leadership development plan, execute the plan, follow-up, and re-assess.

In reality, they need to bring together the key components discovered in this research. The church in revitalization is like a church plant, except it has people and a building, both of which can be a blessing or not. The road forward for each is similar. The components of future success have been identified. Now the components must be assembled and applied.

The knowledge that the research not only affected church plants but also affected churches in revitalization was much more than expected. The scope of the research was limited, but the results have a far-reaching effect on churches in their situation. There is a need to identify what key components are present and which ones are missing and find them. The key components, coupled with a Count the Cost process, for churches in need of revitalization have the capability to change how churches do business.

Lesson Learned: Reaction Was Mixed Regarding the New Ideas

I was very excited about the results of the research project and could not wait to implement what I had learned with new church plants and revitalization churches. I felt I had something very important to share. The reaction was not one that was expected but proved to be a valuable lesson learned.

The new church plants and the church planting schools on the horizon for FBCW were the first places I went to begin to implement what I learned. The church planting process already comprised of Count the Cost and several of the key components. Adding the remaining pieces strengthened the church planting system that already had a good success rate.

Once the church planters heard the results of the research and what I wanted to do going forward, they were excited as well. They saw the benefit of the experience of the successful church planters and wanted that experience to be incorporated into their church plant. Several new churches have been launched since the research project concluded. Each is equipped with the key components discovered. All are off to a great start, with the future looking bright.

The revitalization churches I have worked with since the research project began did not receive the concepts I was sharing at first. I was asked by three churches in need of revitalization to lead a consultation process with them to see if they could turn around. I agreed to work with them.

The first thing we did was to identify the issues that had brought them from a growing and thriving church to one near death. In each church, the issues discovered were basically the same and could be directly linked to the lack of the key components identified in the research project. I was pretty excited because I knew what the church needed.

The push-back came when people in the churches needing revitalization did not want to accept what they had identified as issues leading to their decline. Since the churches would not acknowledge the issues, they did not want to hear about a solution. The churches seemed content to stay in their state until death occurred.

Lack of Understanding of the Biblical Mission of the Church

Fortunately they agreed to move forward and put their apprehension aside. In each church, the number 1 issue identified related to the fact the leaders and the members did not have a clear understanding of the biblical mission of the church. The churches were not sure of the vision and mission for which they existed.

Without them having any understanding of the mission of the church and the direction it should go, decisions were made based on their personal desires or on the basis of their ability to persuade. Needless to say, some bad decisions were made and then compounded by other bad decisions trying to correct the first decision. A culture of bad choices developed over time.

A study of the biblical mission of the church revealed that decisions must be based upon what the Bible says and within the context of why the church existed. At this point some people saw the inevitable end of their reign in the church and pushed back. Some who rejected the biblical concept sought out other churches to attempt to set up a new reign. Others saw the potential of the church when making decisions based on the biblical mission of the church and remained throughout the process.

Lack of Leadership

The next issue identified by all three churches was leadership. The revitalization churches had a dearth of leaders not unlike many churches in the same situation. The church had given leadership to people who did not understand what leadership entailed. The church was adrift with no rudder.

Leadership proved to be the most important component in the research project. The successful church plants had a leader who could articulate a clear vision of where the church was heading and how it might get there. The unsuccessful church plants listed the lack of leadership as their most critical missing component.

Leadership has also proven to be at the heart of each of the revitalization churches. Each church engaged in a rigorous ten-month process of dealing with the identified issues. Part of that was a large gathering where people were asked questions designed to allow them to develop a leadership process for their church.

In each case, the course the church was about to take looked much different than it looked prior to the consultation. In two of the three churches, the pastor, and in one of the cases, the other staff resigned sometime in the ten-month process. I appreciated their honesty and candor. The pastors stated they wanted the best for their church but they felt they were not the ones to take the church on the journey that had been outlined.

Leadership once again cannot be minimized. The development of leaders is crucial to the ongoing health of the church. Leaders are at various levels in their skills and confidence. Securing the right leader for the revitalization churches was critical for their future. Fortunately, the churches called good men with vision to bring biblical leadership to the church.

Lesson Learned: A Teachable Spirit Is Essential

The research project taught me that a teachable spirit is essential if the church is to achieve the mission God has set forth. Each of the successful church planters had a quiet confidence without being arrogant. The church plants that were unsuccessful were led, in some cases, by people who thought they had all the answers and would not listen to anyone else. Others were led by someone with uncertainty regarding call and vision.

The churches in the research succeeded or failed based on leadership, but not just any leadership. The leaders who exhibited humility and a teachable spirit succeeded, while the ones not willing to listen to the counsel of others, for whatever reason, failed. First Baptist Church, Woodstock, does not support the arrogant and the proud, but rather, churches are planted with humble and teachable men.

The Woodstock Church Planting School has had more than 3,400 people from twenty-three countries attend in the first five years of its existence. Many came to the school with a very arrogant attitude and soon found out they did not have all the answers. Those who became teachable have done very well, while those retaining their arrogance have struggled.

Lesson Learned: Focus Is Vital

The research project taught me the importance of focus. The successful church planters were very focused on a few things in particular but never more than they could give time, attention, and clear focus. Unsuccessful church planters did not seem to possess the same sense of focus but rather went from one thing to the next in rapid fire and never focused on any one thing for long.

An F-15 fighter pilot speaking of his training shared that without focus, he dies. In his line of work, there is no room for error. He must focus on the mission and only the mission. He stated, "You can execute better than anyone else in the world, but if you execute against (focus on) the wrong things, you will still lose."

Focus has become a tenant we teach our church planters. Church planters must focus on doing the right things, or they shall surely die.

Reaching people with the Good News is their highest priority, yet often, that is not the focus of many church planters. They instead substitute a lesser priority and expend their limited time, energy, and resources on important things, but not the top priority.

For example, a church planter goes to a community to start a church, and in his mind the top priority is to build a website rather than engage people. Let's say he spends eight hours on his website rather than spending an hour each with eight new families. Both are important, but face-to-face contact with eight new families will likely achieve more than the web-site. Not too many non-believers wake up on Sunday morning and search the web for a new church with few people meeting in a school, where they can go and feel awkward.

Revitalization churches are guilty as well of focusing on things that are not the most important priority for the church. Each church must answer for how they treat personnel, facilities, ministry, and missions. Personnel or facilities or both consume the revitalization church's time, energy, and resources. The church has long since ceased doing missions and ministry.

Unsuccessful plants and revitalization churches have their priorities confused, and until they get them right, the downward spiral will continue. The revitalization church once experienced significant growth when the focus was on reaching people. The downward spiral began when maintaining a building or retaining staff became more important than reaching people.

Lesson Learned: Time Must Be Given to Contemplation

As I wrap up this section on lessons learned, I would be remiss if I did not share what I learned about taking time to contemplate what God is doing. The church planters in the research project were instrumental in teaching me the importance of reflection and allowing God time to speak into my life. Successful church planters were focused but took time to get away and reflect and hear afresh from God. Unsuccessful church planters were always doing something, anything, and did not take time away.

In the church planting school, we teach the basics of church planting on a very significant and practical level. The school has been a blessing to literally thousands who have attended. One thing lacking has now been added to the curriculum, namely, taking time to let God speak to you and your spouse as much as he speaks to you about the church.

A good friend of mine planting a church shared his story regarding this issue. He has been a very successful church planter, has grown his church, built buildings, started other churches, but came to a point with his wife where something needed to change. He had been all about growing the church to the point where the church had become his mistress. He almost sacrificed his family for the church. That must not happen.

He saw the need for him and his wife to take time to contemplate what God was doing and strengthen their relationship. They made changes in their relationship and set boundaries for their home and church life. Their relationship is now strong, and the church continues to grow.

I learned our process was lacking in teaching church planters the importance of setting aside time, when phones and computers are turned off, to simply focus on their relationship with God, their spouse, and the church. The wives attending the school seem to appreciate that section more than any other aspect of the school. The church planter can gain some sense of purpose from his job, but oftentimes, the wife is left at home with the kids and feels alone and left out.

The majority of church planters will not start with multiple staff. More than likely, it will be the church planter, his spouse and children, and maybe another family or two. The church planter may wish for a team, but he needs to realize he already has a team made up of him and his spouse.

Things Taught as a Result of Lessons Learned

Several things are now taught in our church planting school to help church planters and spouses understand their journey together. First of all, the move to a new location will be more challenging than expected. Whether it is across town or across the country, the move will take more out of you than you think it will.

Doctors tell us that a major move is one of the greatest stressors we can encounter. Add to the move the fact that the church planter and his spouse are leaving family and friends and taking a new job, and stress goes off the chart. Church planters, feeling invincible, will cavalierly shrug off the obvious and oftentimes face deep depression soon after arrival on the field.

Second, the road ahead will be lonelier than expected. It is one thing to be in the middle of nowhere and feel lonely, but it is possible to be lonely in a major city. In that time of loneliness, the couple must rely on each other to get through it. The only constant is the relationship with your spouse. Loneliness is a by-product of church planting, in the early stages of the journey at least.

Third, the strain on the relationship will be greater than expected. All relationships face some type of stress and strain. A church planter's strain will be exponentially higher. The church planter and his spouse are away from family and friends for possibly the first time. Family is far away. Financial pressures, even with partnership, will affect the relationship to some degree.

Church planters must recognize their spouse as a valuable team member, because they are. Church planters must respect her role in the church plant. In many ways, it is more important than that of the church planter.

Church planters must carve out time away from the church to be with their spouse. Church planters must find a way for her to regularly spend time with her family.

Our children were born in our South Dakota church plant. Cell phones that could take pictures and face-time did not exist. It was difficult for the grandparents not to hear the first words or see the first steps of their grandchildren.

Pam and I agreed then, whenever we would become grandparents, she would visit the grandchildren at least once each quarter. Cost did not matter. What mattered was she was there for those special times.

Church planters must lift up their spouses not only at home but also in public. Church planters must find time to pray and play with their spouses. Church planters must grasp the importance of the family relationship.

The relationship in the home is only second to a relationship with God. I have learned the importance of that relationship in a deeper way through the research project. Steps have been taken to strengthen the marriage relationship. I am grateful God allowed me to learn this truth and do something about it.

PART TWO

Implications and Ramifications
of the Research Project

CHAPTER SIX

Implications of the Research Project

In part two of this book, I want to explore the implications and impact of the data discovered in this research project. I then want to draw conclusions and address next steps. With new knowledge comes the need to address the question of, *"What now?"*

In part 1, the data discovered in the project was shared, leading to the assumption that enhanced predictability is possible. Not only is enhanced predictability possible, but it also has the capability of completely changing the landscape of church planting. Virtually every aspect of church planting as we know it can be affected by the data in this research project.

The Count the Cost process and the identification of the key components leading to an enhanced predictability of success highlighted part 1. They represented the quantitative and qualitative aspects needed for the project to achieve its purpose. These two areas contain what allows an average person to achieve great things.

Church planting, as pointed out at the beginning of this book, is a relatively new term, with several aspects related to it. Great strides have been made with better theological education, coaching, training, assessments, and partnership. Each one has proven to be very valuable to the church planting process, but the group is certainly more than the sum of its parts. I want to celebrate every aspect that has been woven into the fabric that is church planting.

Is There Room for Additional Aspects of Improvement to Be Introduced into the Church Planting System?

It has taken many years to see the improvements in church planting become main-stream and be supported by a growing number of pastors, churches, and denominational entities. The question seems to be, if another component were to be added to the church planting tool belt suggesting the ability to predict to a much greater degree the future success of church plants, how would it be received? How would it become a part of the main-stream set of church planting tools?

Every level of the church planting process has implications in light of the data contained in the research project. I want to explore briefly what some of the implications could be for the church planting future, beginning with implications for me. I serve as the minister of church planting for FBCW, a church with a desire to see strong churches planted in the under-served places where the number of evangelical witness is very small. After addressing implications for me, I will deal with implications for FBCW, and continue moving outward in a larger and larger circle, concluding with denominational entities.

Implications for Me as a Minister of Church Planting

Believing that enhanced predictability of success is possible affects the way I go about doing what I do. I want to see healthy, reproducing churches birthed with the greatest possibility of success as possible. I also want to see existing churches experience revitalization and become effective once again.

Success happens when the new church or revitalization church is able to affect its community and ultimately reproduce. The focus is not numerical but achieving that for which the church was started. Fulfilling the biblical mission of the church would allow both church plants and revitalization churches to affect the kingdom.

I have been fortunate to have had access to Count the Cost and a practical knowledge of the key components discovered in the research project. The churches I have personally planted contained the key components in large enough quantity to bring success. I now see the need to share the details of enhanced predictability of success with others.

FBCW conducts an ongoing church planting school. As of this writing, over 3,400 people from twenty-three countries have attended the school. The attendees are made up of very different people, different languages, different styles, different contexts and cultures yet are all potentially successful church planters. Each one has the potential to make a difference, but what is the difference maker?

Implication for Me: Every Person Is a Potential Successful Church Planter

An implication of the research project for me is that every person attending the school is a potential successful church planter. The qualities and character of the church planter weigh heavily in the success or failure of the church plant. The system to which the church planter is exposed also plays a key role. The system contains the key components leading to enhanced predictability of success.

The research project, although limited in its scope, contained church planters of every type and level of skill. The average church planter who might have struggled mightily on his own was able to be successful partly because of the key components. The implication points to the recognition that the combination of the leader and the key components enhances the predictability of success for the church plant.

Implication for Me: A Greater Sense of Excitement and Confidence

Another implication for me is that I can approach my work with a greater sense of excitement and confidence. I have made Count the Cost and the assembly of the key components part of the preparation for future church plants. I have great expectation that I will see our church plants continue to grow up and reproduce.

Implication for FBC Woodstock: If Predicting Church Planting Success Is Possible, Then It Could Increase the Church's Desire to Plant More Churches

The belief that predicting church planting success is possible has several implications for FBCW. First of all, it increases the church's desire to plant more churches. The church believes, based on their track record and the data discovered in the research project, that 95 percent of all the churches started with the key components and the Count the Cost process in place will succeed. Again, success is defined as the church achieving the mission God has for it. That confidence energizes the church to plant more churches.

If Predicting Church Planting Success Is Possible, Then It Could Increase the Number of Potential Church Planters

Second, the church suddenly has a much greater pool of church planting candidates from which to choose. The research pointed out that there was not one particular type of person who could successfully plant a church. The case studies involved all different types of people, from highly extroverted to the highly introverted.

The implication is that anyone with a call from God can have a much-enhanced predictability of success. A large portion of the church planters FBCW sends out are members of the church before becoming church planters. All the church planters FBCW supports have attended the FBCW Church Planting School.

A great need exists for qualified church planters moving forward. If there are no limits on the type of person God might call, the implication is that more people in our church will heed God's call in their life. By removing the limiting factors, more FBCW people will seriously consider church planting. The number in the years ahead has the potential to soar.

Helping potential church planters see the church planting journey can be successfully done has the potential for more people to seek the Lord about serving as a church planter. Church planting carries with it a reputation for its challenges to success. The ability to address each of those challenges and how to overcome them has great implications for the future.

Implication for FBCW: Enhanced Predictability Leads to Better Stewardship

Another implication for FBCW involves stewardship. The church would be more eager to provide resources if the predictability of success was greatly enhanced. The church is very generous now and the church planting efforts are solid, but if the predictability of success could be greater, the resources would flow more quickly and in greater amounts. A need always exists and must be filled.

Enhanced Predictability Leads to Better Partnership

Greater success brings more attention and more people into the church planting process. An implication for FBCW would be a much greater involvement by church members and potential partners. Success breeds success. People want to be part of something when they have a great anticipation of its success.

FBCW believes in partnership. If one of our church planters approaches a potential partner and can show that potential partner that the key components of success are in place, coupled with Count the Cost, there is a greater predictability that potential partner will participate. The potential partner will have in front of him a track record of success and know the church planter has done what Luke 14:28 commands.

Implications for Potential Church Planters

For many years potential church planters have endured the horror stories that other church planters shared. Families were often torn apart. Ministries were destroyed for a life-time. The sad aspect is that these stories were true.

Potential church planters hesitated to step out on their own. In the early days of church planting, the church planter did not have the knowledge or the tools he has today. No system existed to let them see the journey ahead or even what the next step should be as they moved forward.

Much like construction, the various pieces must be assembled in the proper order. Failure to do so puts the project at risk. At best it must be taken apart and reassembled, costing time and money.

Church planters without a process illustrating for them the next steps found they were going back and re-evaluating some of their earlier decisions and projects. Church planters have a limited time-frame and limited resources to apply to the church plant. Any extra money or time needed to accomplish the task can be fatal in the long run.

Implication for Church Planters: The Ability to See Into the Future Could Make the Church Planter More Effective

What if a church planter could see the future and know what to do next? He could be much more efficient and much more purposeful in his daily tasks. He could spend his time on building relationships and sharing vision rather than fixing a problem caused by a lack of understanding of the journey.

If a church planter could view the future, he could see where the dangers on the journey lie and adjust to avoid the problem. He could see when and how many leaders must be trained to minister effectively. He would understand his need to provide space and leadership at the right time or lose the window of opportunity.

An implication for church planters, related to the data discovered in the research project, rests in the fact that with the data and the Count the Cost process, it is possible for the church planter to look into the future. He can see the next step. He can see the dangers. He can see what the decisions he is about to make would look like when they grew up.

Seeing decisions come to fruition can be a blessing or a very scary time in the life of the church planter. He has two choices as a result of the data discovered in the research project. He can make decisions now and live them out and take his chances knowing some decisions might be fatal, or he can utilize Count the Cost and the key components and see the results of his decisions projected right in front of him.

The church planter sees the results of his decisions projected to maturity and is able to make changes to his decisions without living through the pain. He is able to save his church plant, his family, and his ministry because nothing fatal can blind-side him. He can have greater confidence and be sure he is on track at all times.

Implication for Church Planters: Enhanced Predictability Produces a Greater Ability to Secure Partners

Another implication for church planters relates to their ability to secure partners. Knowing how much is needed and for how long is essential in securing partners. Having the means to show a potential partner the trajectory of the church plant's growth pattern and support, along with ministry plans designed to reach people and make disciples of people, gives the church planter a definitive edge over church planters who cannot share that information with the potential partner.

Church planters, by their very nature, are not necessarily concerned with the nuts and bolts of church planting. They want to preach and not take the time it takes to understand the process. The research project data provides a simple, picture-like view of the process and allows the church planter to do what needs to be done with a lesser knowledge and a lesser amount of time than if the process is not available.

Implication for Church Planters: Enhanced Predictability Produces a Greater Confidence the Church Plant Will Succeed

Another implication for the church planter from the research project is that he and his family can have a greater degree of confidence the church will succeed. If 95 percent of any venture was successful, one can have extreme confidence the portion of the whole he possesses will be successful. Not to succeed would be the exception.

Church planters and their spouses face great fear as they prepare for the church plant to start. Planting a church for each of them is a definite unknown. How will they survive financially? How will this move affect their relationship? How will the kids adjust? All are valid questions that can be answered with the data found in the research project.

The church planting highway does not need to be a washed-out, rut-filled, bumpy adventure. It does not have to be viewed as danger around every turn. The road can be made smoother and straighter and navigable. The ability to see several miles down the road travelled increases the possibility to arrive safely at the desired destination. Increasing how far down the road the church planter can see improves the predictability of success.

All this may sound very unspiritual and leaning more toward the practical. The church planting universe is filled with "ten biblical reasons why you should plant a church", and other theological and biblical training. This process leans unashamedly toward the practical. This process is primarily designed to help the church planter make the journey safely and successfully.

In the road trip analogy, churches are not dying at the point of assessment. Churches are not dying at the point of launch. Churches are dying somewhere on the journey, blind-sided by something they did not see coming, but could have seen with a process that points out the danger zones in place.

Theology, missiology, and ecclesiology are all important but are to no avail if the church plant dies because the church planter failed to sit down and think through the process. Keeping the church planter alive and serving also allows him to live out his theology. Both are essential. It is the chicken and the egg again. Yet, the amount of practical, on-the-journey, training is very much limited in church planting circles today.

Implications for Partnering Churches

The research project held implications for me in my ministry, for the church I serve, and for church planters. Another group with significant implications is the partnering or sending churches. These churches are the lifeblood of the ministry of church planting. Without partners and sending churches, church planting would go back thirty years.

Sadly, statistics tell us that approximately 4 percent of churches are involved in any way in planting a church. The question I ask is "why?" Why are there not more churches joining together to see new life spring forth? Why are churches content with mere existence when there is a better way?

Honestly, I do not have the answer to the questions. I surmise that fear of failure has much to do with it. First, pastors fear failure for their church. Many churches in revitalization I work with have done all they know and have not seen growth. They fear attempting to start a church would be the final straw leading to the death of their church.

Second, pastors fear the church plant will not be successful. If they have not seen successful church plants personally, they know of someone who tried to start a church only to have it fail. They are now not willing to take the risk again since the journey of church planting is so difficult to navigate.

Third, pastors feel it will cost more than it really does. A few years before I became the director of missions in Phoenix, one church had planted another church single-handedly. The sending church was strong. The new church grew up and was strong. The birth and development of the new church cost a great deal and was borne by the sending church.

My desire was to see many churches birthed, but the concept of partnership was the way I wanted to accomplish it. I asked the sending pastor if he would be the sending church for another church plant. He thought back to his previous experience and what it cost and was hesitant at that point.

I introduced him to partnership, and he saw what each church needed to contribute to the church plant. When he saw the number, he said that his church would be a partner in two church plants. A partnership movement began and continues to this day.

Implication for Partnering Churches: Enhanced Predictability Overcomes Fear

An implication for sending churches and partner churches based on the research project addresses the issue of fear. If indeed fear of some sort is the reason more churches do not partner, what if the fear could be eliminated and replaced with confidence? Removal of fear is the implication.

If fear is gone because a greater degree of predictability exists, more churches will be willing to partner. The fact that key components identified in the research project can be assembled along with a Count the Cost process means that much of the unknown that causes fear can be eliminated. The landscape of church planting partnerships could be changed forever.

The sending church or the partner churches can see the picture of the journey with its danger points and see what the church planter will do to address the dangers. The sending church and partner churches will see other churches in similar situations, seeing success. Quiet confidence is a wonderful thing to have in an ever-changing situation.

Implication for Partnering Churches: Enhanced Predictability Improves Stewardship

Another implication for sending churches and partners involves stewardship. Every church desires to be good stewards of what God places in their care. In my experience, churches have been hesitant to get involved in church planting because they felt they could not afford it. In their mind it would be a constant drain well into the future.

With the process outlined in the research project, a church can know how much and how long its support will be needed. A reasonable growth pattern establishes a built-in sunset on the church's support to the church plant. The church, while showing generosity, is also a good steward since the amount needed is shared by many partners and not borne solely by the sending church.

Implication for Partnering Churches: Enhanced Predictability Promotes Accountability

Another implication based on the research project for sending churches and partnering churches surrounds the topic of accountability. Every church plant needs accountability. The church planter and the church plant are at high risk without a high level of accountability. The church planters in the research project all pointed to accountability as one of the keys to their success. Also, lack of accountability brought some churches down and caused their demise.

Accountability not only for the church planter but also accountability between partnering churches is essential. Each successful church plant had a partnership covenant clearly outlining the expectations of each partner. The partners would agree and sign off on the covenant. Once in place, each partner was held to his commitment.

Implications for Church Planting Catalysts, Directors of Missions, and Other Facilitators of Church Planting and Church Planting Networks

I served as director of missions for approximately ten years. One of my passions involved church planting. The association of churches where I served contained three churches involved in church planting with a very limited budget to assist in planting churches. Yet, I was determined to see what God might do in the coming years. Over the next ten years, many churches became sending churches and partnering churches. The partnership mentality is still a vital part of the association.

The role of the church planting catalyst or the director of missions, or even the facilitator of church planting can be very difficult. Every church planter believes the church he will plant is the most important in the world and will be extremely successful. The church planting catalyst, director of missions, and the facilitator must filter through all the excitement and find out if the church plant is viable or not. Every church plant looks good in someone's mind.

Let me give an example: I receive many prospectuses from church planters. They look something like the following: thirty pages with full-color photos. Keep in mind the cost of the document and the fact that it is shared by someone who is there to ask me for money.

The first fourteen pages are telling me the place where he will plant his church is filled with people who do not know Jesus as Savior and Lord. This is all nice, expensive information, but I already know the place he is planting his church is filled with unbelievers. I could say that about every city and hamlet in America.

The last fourteen pages are telling me his church is going to be planting multiple churches every year. The problem is that very little is given in the two pages in the middle to show me how the church will grow, develop, and make the transition from new start to flourishing church planting center. I have little to go on, and my decision-making process may be flawed.

Implication for CPCs, DOMs, and Facilitators: Provides the Ability to Vet Viability

An implication for CPCs, DOMs, and facilitators of church planting, based on data from the research project, is that it provides a way to vet the data in the church planter's prospectus and determine if the church is viable or not. Not every church plant is viable. In some cases, the information is lacking to make a clear analysis, but with Count the Cost and the key components in place, a clear determination can be made about the future of the church plant.

Implication for CPCs, DOMs, and Facilitators: Provides a Training Opportunity

Another implication for CPCs, DOMs, and facilitators of church planting is that the data in the research project helps them know how to train a church planter in what to present to potential partners. This aspect is extremely important. The church planters coming to me for help need someone to help them prepare for our meeting to talk about partnership.

Based on the data in the research project, the successful church planters had the best results when it came to partner support. The following are some of the things they mentioned regarding meeting with partners:

- Be as professional as possible. Do not just drop in on a potential partner. His schedule is probably already full. If you just drop by, you may create the feeling that you do not respect his time. He may want to give you all the time needed, but in an unplanned few minutes, he may not be able to do so. You must make the most of every potential partner meeting.
- Be able to articulate your key message clearly and with high resolution. Do not waste time with inconsequential information. The potential partner is meeting with you to determine whether he will support you or not, so stick with the pertinent information.
- Be concise as well as precise with your presentation. Put your presentation into an elevator speech and deliver it with heart-felt passion. You basically have from the first floor to the fifth floor to gain the attention of the potential partner and want him to hear more.
- When you go to an appointment, always bring the presentation in writing even though you have sent it earlier. The potential partner's desk may be full, and you do not want him to have to hunt for your information. Always introduce yourself through your preparation before you introduce yourself in person.
- Be sure you respect the time of the potential partner. If the meeting is scheduled for thirty minutes, take twenty. If it is

an hour, take forty-five minutes. Never violate the timeline. Respect the timeline and you will be respected. Abuse the timeline and you may sacrifice your opportunity.

- Be sure your documents and presentation are of quality and error-free. Make your presentation the best it can be on the budget available. Have several people check it over and have them give you an honest opinion.
- Be aware of the timeline of the potential partnering church's budget. Know when the partnering church budget begins and when the information needs to be in his hand to present for the next budget year. Failure to know these important facts may cause the loss of support even though the potential partner church wants to help.
- Be courteous and understand the potential partner has been through this process before. He is doing what he is doing because he knows what he is looking for in your presentation. Do not try to manipulate or coerce the potential partner in any way. Do not try to *guilt-trip* the potential partner into helping you.
- Be aware of the DNA of the potential partnering church. For example, First Baptist Church, Woodstock, has a desire to plant churches in what is called the "under-served" areas. These are areas with very limited evangelical witness. If you are planning to plant your church in a very churched area where the evangelical witness is high, chances are I will not be supporting you. I will more than likely support a church plant in a difficult and under-served area of the country.
- Be honest and always tell the truth. It is too easy to find out if you are not telling the truth. If you are found by the potential partner to have not been honest with him, you will lose not only his support but also the support of everyone in his network. The necessity of honesty cannot be overstated.
- Be aware that dropping names does not mean anything to the potential partner. He does not care who you know nearly as much as what you plan to do. He wants you to tell him your story and your "*future picture*." He must see what you see and feel what you feel, or he will not form the connection necessary to support you.

- Be sure to practice full disclosure as it relates to other partners. If you need $1,000, the potential partner needs to know what other partners are in play and what they have contributed. If $1,000 is needed and five churches send $1,000 each, that is dishonest and, once found out, will end your support and possibly your ministry.

- Be careful not to bite the hand that is about to feed you. If the potential partner is from a traditional-style church, do not make disparaging remarks about his church. His style may not be for you, but show the respect to a church willing to take a chance on you.

- Be certain the words *"thank you,"* are in your vocabulary. The ladies Bible study class in a church of thirty that sends $10 each month deserves the same appreciation and thankful attitude as the church that gives much more. When you find yourself on the platform, speaking, just realize you did not get there alone. Thank-you needs to become a part of your DNA. The simple words, *thank you*, go a long way in strengthening relationships.

An implication of the research project involves understanding what and how to ask for support from potential partners. Finding and securing partners does not just happen. It is a skill that must be learned by potential church planters early in the church planting process.

Implications for Denominational Entities Based on the Research

Denominational entities have a great deal of influence on the field of church planting and have been instrumental in moving the dial forward with church planting success. Church planting is more visible than it has been in my lifetime due to the positive influence of the denominational entities. Each one deserves their just due for what has been accomplished.

The data uncovered in the research project could be added to the denominational tool belt to help church planters become even more effective. The data provides a real-time situation where success is happening as well as an answer as to why it is happening. Nothing needs changing, but something could be added that would make a long-term difference in the success of new church plants.

Implication for Denominational Entities: Provides a Means and Method to Help Church Planters

An implication for denominational entities focuses on their willingness to seek out new means and methods to help church planters build their church. It appears in recent years there is a willingness to try new things and utilize new things developed in the field. The data in the research project added to what is already in place would add greatly to the enhanced predictability of church planting success.

Denominational entities also have a great deal of influence on churches in need of revitalization. Many churches I have worked with have lost their way over the years and are not certain what they are supposed to do. The biblical mission of the church has been lost. The church plants and the churches in need of revitalization are in need of the same components identified in the research project. The data could be very helpful along with the Count the Cost process to assist churches to recapture the vision God gave the church. The principals involved in planting a church and those involved in revitalizing a church are two sides of the same coin.

Implication for Denominational Entities: Provides Additional Avenues of Preparation for Church Planters

Another implication for denominational entities based on the research project involves the priorities of church planter preparation. The primary preparation includes an assessment of the church planter. Much about his call, family life, and vision are explored thoroughly.

The focus is on the church planter and his ability, or lack thereof, to plant successfully.

The data in the research project points out that while the church planter is crucial, other components assembled at the start of the church plant have a dramatic impact on the success of the church plant. Going forward, would it be beneficial to the denominational entities to add the identification and compilation of the key components to the preparation of the church planters? I believe it would behoove the entities to explore the possibility.

Along the same line, assembling the key components leading to enhanced predictability for revitalization churches would begin with leadership. The possibility of a pool of trained pastors with the knowledge of the key components and their importance would be of great benefit. Once the leader is in place, other aspects of the research project will apply, including call, vision, plan, partnership, and realistic expectations.

Implication for Denominational Entities: Provides A Means of Accountability

Another implication for denominational entities based on the research project deals with accountability. The research project proved the value and importance of accountability for the church planters and other partners. Every successful church planter listed the immense importance of accountability in his church plant.

The denominational entities need a universal way to keep up with the church planters regularly. The front lines of ministry are very long and the support personnel are few compared to what is needed for ongoing support. The denominational entities might want to consider a Count the Cost process with the church plants to allow for a universal and systematic accountability.

Count the Cost breaks down the church planter's journey into months with specific and realistic goals to be achieved based on the church planter's knowledge of his field of ministry. The church planter and the denominational entity both have a copy so that all parties are on the same page. Simple questions allow the entity to "coach" the church planter at least every month and hold him accountable for the agreed-upon outcomes.

Far too often, contact with the church planter is too spread out to be effective. A contact in one month and not until several months later can spell disaster. If something goes wrong or if a problem arises, unless the church planter makes the contact with the entity, the whole scenario may play out without any input from anyone else.

If ongoing contact could be established early in the planting process, many problems that may prove fatal may be averted. The church planter can be saved a trauma in his life and ministry. His family may not have to endure the pain and anguish accompanying a crisis event alone.

Implication for Denominational Entities: Provides for Realistic Expectations

Another implication for denominational entities based on the data discovered in the research project revolves around realistic expectations. The denominational entities must find a way to apply principles rather than blanket application. The research project clearly showed that realistic expectations were vital to the success of the new church plants.

The successful church planters understood their field of ministry and could ascertain what a reasonable growth pattern might be for that area. After setting a realistic goal, each church planter had a target to hit and could be held to that standard. Each successful church planter exceeded his projection but stated it was important that it was reachable to begin the church plant. An unrealistic goal can be demoralizing and detrimental to the church plant if with their best effort the goal is unattainable.

Summary of Implications

The previous pages point to implications to individuals, church planters, sending churches, partnering churches, facilitators of church plants, and denominational entities regarding how the data from the research project could possibly affect the future. The implications listed here certainly are not exhaustive but rather indicators of possibilities. The possibilities for enhanced predictability found in these and other implications are attainable.

The research project has the possibility of great impact on many areas of the process called church planting. The question remains: "Will the data discovered in the research project leading to enhanced predictability for success of future church plants be accepted?" Many good ideas and good studies are often ignored or rejected outright. My prayer is that this concept will get an audience and a fair hearing.

The research project also has implications for churches in revitalization. Much is being done to bring the crisis of non-growing Southern Baptist churches to light. Much is also being done to challenge churches that need revitalization to seek help from churches desiring to assist the revitalization churches.

The issue currently is basically *"What now?"* What are the steps that must be taken to begin a revitalization process? Where does the church start? Based on the research project, a process has been developed and field-tested with amazing results. The following gives an overview of that process.

The Ultimate Outcomes Desired

The church will have a clear snapshot of where it currently stands regarding the centrality of God's Word, evangelism, discipleship, organization, mission, worship, hospitality, financial stability, and member care.

- The church will have a clear understanding of its structure, faith and practice, and financial obligations.
- The church will be able to see a clear picture of a preferred future based on the Count the Cost process, which will guide the steps taken in the future.
- The church will know and understand the "next step" in its life-cycle.
- The church will have analyzed the key issues discovered in the questionnaire and drawn conclusions regarding any changes needed to achieve the vision.
- The church will have designed and implemented plans to achieve the goals laid out in the process.

Steps and Timeline to Achieve the Desired Outcomes

Month #1

- Meet with key leaders to identify for them the data needed to design a Count the Cost for the church. This will provide a real-time snapshot of the condition of the church at the beginning of the process.
- Meet again with the key leaders to share with them their unique Count the Cost process.

Month #2:

- Have the church complete the eighty question questionnaire to determine key issues. The key leaders will complete the questionnaire separately from the congregation to see if the key leaders and church members are on the same page and seeing things the same.

- Take a look at the overall structure of the church to determine what steps, if any, must be taken to align with the criteria in the Count the Cost process.
- Meet with the pastor and key leaders and update them on the results of the survey. Point out significant findings. Discuss the structure of the church and what next steps are needed to be considered.

Month #3:

- Have the church and the key leaders complete the threats-and-opportunities questionnaire consisting of two questions.
- Meet with the pastor and key leaders to update them on the results of the threats-and-opportunities questionnaire.
- Discuss the top three or four key issues and determine the order in which they will be addressed.
- Begin discussing the first key issue and how it is playing out in the church as we begin.
- Set a time for a consultant report on a Sunday morning in the next month or so.

Month #4:

- Discuss the key issues in the church further, asking the pastor and key leaders for their input regarding each key issue and how they see it surfacing in the church.
- Set the dates for a meeting with the congregation to begin to design and implement ministry plans to address the key issues.

Month #5:

- Meet with the pastor and key leaders to give them the process you will use with the church members to design and develop the first ministry plan.
- Meet with as many of the congregation that will come to design and determine the best way to implement a ministry plan to deal with their first key issue.
- Meet with the pastor and key leaders to assess and debrief the ministry plan developed by the people.

Month #6:

- Meet with the pastor and key leaders to give them the process you will use with the church members to design and develop the second ministry plan.
- Meet with as many of the congregation that will come to design and determine the best way to implement a ministry plan to deal with their second key issue.
- Meet with the pastor and key leaders to assess and debrief the ministry plan developed by the people.

Month #7:

- Meet with the pastor and key leaders to give them the process you will use with the church members to design and develop the third ministry plan.
- Meet with as many of the congregation that will come to design and determine the best way to implement a ministry plan to deal with their third key issue.
- Meet with the pastor and key leaders to assess and debrief the ministry plan developed by the people.

(At this point, the pastor and key leaders could choose to take all eight issues to the people, which would add to the timeline.)

Month #8:

- Meet with the pastor and key leaders to discuss the process and next steps.
- Review the Count the Cost process to see if the church has progressed as anticipated.
- Re-examine the ultimate outcomes expected to determine if the church has accomplished all the goals.
- Plan for a consultant report on a Sunday morning to share with the entire congregation what the leadership and the church members have done over the past nine months or so.

Month #9:

- Meet with the pastor and key leaders to share what you will be bringing to the church.
- Make the consultant's report to the congregation, sharing with them what the leadership and the church members have done.

(At this point the pastor and key leaders may determine if they want to extend the process to include three months up to six months of coaching through the implementation process.)

Month #10:

- Finalize all report and action plans. Provide the church with all documentation gathered and developed during the process.

This process has been field-tested and has proven to be very effective in helping churches in need of revitalization. The church gets a Count the Cost evaluation indicating a real-time status of the church's health and growth capacity moving forward. Without this real-time evaluation, it becomes difficult to gauge progress.

The church is able to determine the real issues leading to the church's decline, possibly for the first time. It is often a shock and very painful for the church to see how it has slipped and given in to decisions furthering its decline. However, once the church faces up to the issues, the process of dealing with those issues can begin.

Dealing with the issues and admitting they exist is only half the battle. The church is then able to design and implement new ministries leading to a new future. It is often here the current pastor finds he is not the person to lead the church forward and resigns. This is not always the case, but it is a reality of revitalization.

The next aspect I want to address will deal with the conclusions drawn from the research. Some conclusions will be very obvious, but some may cause the reader of this book to pause and ponder for a moment. Should that occur, the book will have been a success.

CHAPTER SEVEN

Conclusions Drawn From
the Research Project

In a research project of any kind, many conclusions may be drawn. This research project is no different. In fact, the topic of this research project raises many questions and calls for many conclusions. Some are obvious, and some are very subtle.

Conclusion: Enhanced Predictability Is Not Only Possible But Also to Be Expected

The premise held at the beginning of the research simply stated, "Is it possible to enhance the predictability of success of future church plants?" Is there a way to ensure a greater possibility the church plant would grow and make an impact on the community where it will be planted? If enhanced predictability is possible, "what components are necessary to ensure enhanced predictability of success?"

Based on the research project, success is not some nebulous entity that can never be possessed. In fact, the components leading to enhanced predictability resemble "a blinding flash of the obvious." Nothing about the successful church plants was mysterious or unattainable.

Church planting, in my experience, is viewed as something only a few people do. It is thought of as more difficult than other ministries of the church, and rightfully so. It is thought to be the destroyer of families and ministries. It is viewed with great skepticism since it does not have a great track record of success.

Church planting, however, can be a very powerful and uplifting experience. The circumstances are difficult at times, but the rewards are also many. In South Dakota, financial support was minimal. One Sunday I told my wife we needed $400 in the offering to provide fuel oil for our boiler, going into winter.

I knew we had already given our tithe, which was far less than what it would take to fill the tank. On that Sunday it rained. A combining crew making their way north was forced to shut down for the day and decided to attend our little church. When the service was over and the offering was counted, there was exactly $400 in the offering. God always comes through and on time.

The results of the research project disprove the prevailing ideas about church planting. Enhanced predictability of success is indeed possible. Key components existed in the church plants that proved to be the key to a successful church planting experience. The key components did not exist in the churches that did not succeed.

The conclusion involves the belief that enhanced predictability is possible when the key components have been secured and assembled. The key components are available and attainable. The key components must be applied early in the life of the church plant.

Conclusion: A Correlation Exists Between Successful Church Plants and the Key Components Enhancing Predictability of Success

At the outset of the research project, I knew the possibility existed that certain components would be discovered that proved to be the game-changer for the church plant. For severe storms to develop, certain elements must be present. I was not surprised that the key components were identified. I was surprised each successful church planter listed the same components. I was equally surprised the unsuccessful church plants held the same key components, but as missing.

Why these key components? Why not others? What do these components provide in combination that they do not provide individually? The elements leading to the development of severe storms demand that several things come together to cause the predictable reaction. The same is true in church planting and revitalization. The combination of these specific key components is necessary to provide the predictable result.

I believed in the possibility of the correlation based on my past history and fascination with weather and predictability. The research project confirmed what I believed but could not prove definitively. It is somewhat comforting to realize what you have believed in your heart all your life is actually true. Even more rewarding than that is the knowledge that what has been discovered has the potential to completely change the church planting landscape.

Conclusion: The Key Components Are Easily Identified

The term that comes to mind to describe the key components would be, "a blinding flash of the obvious." There is nothing strange or exotic about the key components. There is nothing rare or unattainable. The key components are common, ordinary things we take for granted every day. We assume the key components exist, when in reality they do not naturally occur.

Leadership to a certain degree is present in everyone but can and must be nurtured and taught to be effective. God's call is not of our doing but is given by God, as is the vision of what he wants us to do. God's call carries with it his vision and the ability to achieve it.

Partnership does not naturally occur. Partnership is a direct result of relationship building over time.

The key components individually are powerful in their own right. Each has the potential and the power to change the circumstances in a dramatic way. Each one makes the church planter or revitalization pastor more effective in achieving God's vision for the future. However, when the key components are in combination, the potential and power are multiplied exponentially.

The key components must be assembled to be effective. It would be nice if they were naturally occurring but they are not. Everyone is not a leader with a call and a vision from God. Partnership does not just happen.

It takes time to build a partnership. Realistic expectations are the exception rather than the rule. The church planter or the sending entity often super-imposes unrealistic expectations leading to ongoing issues.

The key components must be nurtured. Like anything of value, the key components, once identified and assembled, must be given time to develop. Leadership is a life-long process where no one ever arrives. There is always more to be learned and applied.

The call of God does not rest on everyone who claims to be a pastor or church planter. While serving at the North American Mission Board, my team had the opportunity to interview more than 2,500 pastors in the field. Two of the questions we asked produced troubling results. The vast majority of pastors in the field did not articulate a call from God or a vision of what God wanted them to do. Assuming the key components exist naturally is a false assumption.

The vision given by God must constantly be clarified and communicated clearly. God's vision is not to be hidden and obscured, but must be clearly stated and executed in the light of God's revelation. Scripture is clear that without vision, people perish. Vision leads to life and fellowship with Jesus.

Partnership is at best very difficult. If it were easy, more than the 4 percent of churches indicated in the NAMB study would be involved in a church planting partnership. Partnership must also be nurtured.

Partnership finds its base in strong relationships built over time. Partnership requires an investment of time and energy by the church planter. The church planter will never have a partnership if he does not make relationship building a very high priority.

The church planter must know his field well enough to determine with a good degree of accuracy what a realistic growth pattern looks like and how it will be achieved. It does no good for the church or the church planter to carry unrealistic expectations. One of the key components identified by the churches in the research project involved establishing realistic expectations.

The fact that the key components are identifiable and ordinary makes it possible for all church plants and revitalization churches to assemble them to enhance predictability of success. Leaders have no excuse for not adding the key components to their process. Adding the key components will enhance their opportunity to succeed.

Conclusion: Results Are Measureable

The ability to have measureable results leads to enhanced predictability. Count the Cost indicates the path the church will follow as it grows. The fact the church planter can know what results are expected is very important for several reasons:

- Measureable results encourage the church planter and all who are part of the church.
- Measureable results indicate what the church planter must do each day to achieve the goals that are three months or even six months away.
- Measureable results provide a level of accountability.

- Measureable results give potential partners a good idea of what to expect if they partner together with the new church.
- Measureable results help the church planter focus on the task at hand and not look further down the road than he should.

In my experience, there has not been enough emphasis on the importance of measureable goals. Church planters talk about reaching their city or reaching the world. Those are good goals, but often, there is not a plan to reach the next five people.

Unless the church reaches the next one, it will not reach the city or the world. Without measureable goals, it is easy to be drawn into the larger picture and lose sight of the one. The shepherd left the ninety-nine and sought after the one.

Several years ago, my wife and I attended a small church. The pastor preached with great zeal and passion. It was obvious he truly believed what he was preaching.

We attended the church for a number of weeks, and each week, the pastor would talk about becoming a church that would reach North Georgia and the world. I was excited to hear a message preached with such conviction and fervor. I wanted to know more about what he was preaching.

The pastor came over to my house after we had attended for several weeks. I asked him to articulate his vision. He began to share and got very excited when he came to the part about reaching North Georgia and the world. He had this aspect of the vision settled in his heart.

I shared with him how much I appreciated his heart and the messages, but I had a question to ask. I asked him what his plans were to reach the next ten people. He seemed caught off guard by the question.

After a while, he admitted he had no plan to reach the next ten people. He had focused on the larger picture. He had no measureable goals to help him focus on reaching people one at a time. It is now ten years later, and his church is the same size it was ten years ago.

One of the traits of the successful church planters in the research project involved a systematic plan to identify people who did not know Jesus. They were very intentional about engaging them, and, ultimately, reaching them, making them disciples, and deploying them in ministry. The vision was based on intentionally focusing on the one who needs Jesus, which will lead to influencing the world.

The key components help the church planter focus on the individual by developing an outreach plan designed to involve as many people in the work of the ministry of evangelism as possible. The church planter cannot rely on nebulous concepts and non-existent goals. Goals and results must be measureable to be effective.

The research project data indicated clearly how important it is to have measureable goals. The successful church planters spend their day focused on a reachable, attainable, and measureable goal. The unsuccessful church planters did not have a plan to address a measureable number of people to achieve a measureable result.

Conclusion: Church Plants Must Have Partnership to Survive

In my South Dakota church planting experience, I was fortunate to have a partnering church, even though what the church provided left a large gap between surviving and thriving. The partnering church made the difference in the success or failure of the work. I could not have survived without their help.

I did my part as well. I hunted, fished, and heated my house with wood. I worked with a funeral director to retrieve the bodies of people who had died, oftentimes ninety or more miles away. I realized partnership involves all parties doing whatever it takes to achieve the agreed-upon outcome.

Thirty-eight years ago it was possible to make it with a single partner. Today it takes many partners to be sure the church planter's needs are met. FBCW seeks to understand the amount actually needed by conducting Count the Cost. Once the number is determined, we desire the church planter to secure that amount of partnership before he starts his new church.

The conclusion drawn from the research data speaks to the extreme need for multiple partnership relationships. Church plants with sufficient partnership succeeded, while those without sufficient resources failed to survive. The key components include adequate partnership for the church to have time to reach enough people whose giving will replace that of the partner churches over time.

Knowing how much and for how long becomes a crucial number for the church planter to know. For example, if the church planter needs to reach 165 people to be self-sufficient over five years, he now knows what to do. The church planter realizes he does not need to reach 400 but rather 165. That number is important to him but also to potential partners.

Partners come in all shapes and sizes. Some will become the sending church taking on the legal responsibility for the new church but also providing significant resources. Others will be supporting churches providing a financial contribution based on the need determined by the Count the Cost process. Still, others will become prayer partners, people partners, and team partners.

All partners are important. None is more valuable than another. Prayer partners or people partners still provide what the church needs that money cannot buy.

Devising a strategy to identify, engage, and utilize partners is essential to the enhanced success of the new church. Partnerships simply do not happen without effort and intentionality. With the absence of clear protocols, articulated expectations, and clear accountability, church planting partnerships are doomed to fail.

I have witnessed partnerships dissolve because somewhere in the process the sending or receiving partner became disappointed or disillusioned. Whether caused by unfulfilled expectations or disagreement over strategic direction, most partnerships fail because some aspects of either partner's expectations were clearly not stated at the beginning. This scenario does not have to happen.

Every church planter needs to develop a process to utilize when engaging partners. One of the key issues a potential partner is concerned about is the church planter and his character. In a partnership, it is important that all parties agree on personal standards of behavior.

FBCW has certain qualities we look for in the church planters with whom we partner. Our partnerships include church planters who are the following:

- humble
- teachable
- high personal integrity
- inspiring
- pure in thoughts, actions, and motives
- passionate
- authentic
- responsible
- articulate

FBCW also looks for certain strategic abilities such as the following:

- Vision: the church planter must possess and passionately articulate a God-given vision.
- Entrepreneurship: the church planter must be creative, resourceful, and a risk-taker.
- Reproductive mentality: the church planter must, at the outset of the church plant, be committed to being able to effectively reproduce his church.
- Leadership: the church planter must be able to effectively develop and execute a strategy and lead a team.
- Effective: the church planter must be able to discern what to give his time, energy, and resources to for him to achieve the greatest result.

FBCW also looks for church planters with professional skills:

- Record of achievement: the church planter should be able to point to past success since past success is the best indicator of future success.
- High morals and character: the church planter must understand that success at any cost is not acceptable. Maintaining biblical standards at all times is a must, and the ends never justify the means.
- Attraction: the church planter must be able to attract other partners.
- Team Leadership: the church planter must realize he cannot do what is needed alone, he must involve, equip, and utilize his team for the good of the kingdom.

FBCW also wants the church planter to fit the context of the church plant. Questions are asked about geography and people groups. It must be determined whether the church planter can function effectively in the context and culture.

Different kinds of partnering relationships have different levels of authority. In some cases, FBCW has a greater involvement in strategic development. In other cases, FBCW takes a more supportive role. FBCW will oftentimes assume a coaching role and, in others, serve as a supervisor.

Ultimately, according to the level of partnership and the needs of the church plant, FBCW will provide varying levels of services. Each church plant is different. FBCW drafts a partnership agreement that is unique to every church plant based on the circumstances and needs. In whatever level FBCW participates in a partnership, there must be clearly articulated and agreed-upon protocols at the beginning of the partnership agreement.

Conclusion: The Church Planting and Revitalization Landscape Can Be Changed

The data discovered in the research project led to another conclusion. The church planting and revitalization landscape can and will hopefully be changed by the data gathered. Churches can be started more effectively. Churches in need of revitalization can have hope that their church will turn around.

The impact of the discovery of the key components leading to the enhancement of predictability of success cannot be minimized. Pastors and church leaders have been trying to discover what could reverse the downward trend of churches all across America. Perhaps the truths and principles gleaned from this research project will be what is needed to make a difference.

Moving forward, sending churches, partnering churches, and church planters can have a greater degree of confidence that the new church will succeed. Revitalization church pastors and men who feel called to serve in revitalization churches can know what is missing from the church and begin to assemble the missing components. By doing so, the way churches are planted and the way churches are being revitalized can be revolutionized.

CHAPTER EIGHT

EVALUATION,... NEXT STEPS,...WHAT NOW?

First Baptist Church, Woodstock, is a great church with a world-wide ministry upon which the sun never sets. FBCW is built around seven major ministries. One of the seven major aspects of the ministry of FBCW is church planting. Recently the revitalization of churches has become part of the church planting ministry.

I have the privilege of leading the church planting ministry and also interfacing with the campus pastors in the church revitalizations. The revitalization churches fall under my ministry since churches in revitalization must begin to think and function like church plants. There is little difference in a church plant and a church in revitalization.

Both entities must re-engage their community and articulate a clear and compelling vision of how the church will minister to the community. The entities must also design relevant ministries to fulfill the vision. Finally, both must follow up on those who feel led to become a part of the work.

I conducted the research project with the desire to see church plants and revitalization churches become a vibrant and effective part of the community in which God had placed them. Personally, I have seen church plants struggle and have sadly seen many die. I have more recently been closely associated with churches struggling to regain what they once possessed, namely, an effective ministry.

The evaluation of the research project must be tied to whether or not church plants have a greater degree of enhanced predictability of success than before the research was conducted. Evaluation is also tied to whether revitalization churches are more effective in turning from a downward trend to an upward trend. The evaluation finally must be based on whether the key components have been identified and how each can be utilized moving ahead.

Evaluation: Do Church Plants Have an Enhanced Predictability of Success?

Based on the research, the church plants incorporating the key components identified in this project evidenced a much-enhanced predictability for success. Identifying the key components allows new church plants to possess a greater knowledge of how to prepare the new church to start. FBCW will implement a stronger church planting process than it did before the research project.

By the criteria listed above, the research project achieved the desired outcome as it relates to church plants. The question now becomes what about the future? Certainly time will tell.

The key components have been identified. The case for enhanced predictability for the success of future church plants has been made. Enhanced predictability is within reach of all future church planters.

Evaluation: Are Revitalization Churches Utilizing the Data from the Research Project, Turning from a Downward Trend to an Upward Trend in Their Journey?

There are basically three possibilities with regard to revitalization:

- The first option of self-revitalization is filled with issues, making it the least successful possibility of all. If the pastor and leaders were going to turn the church around, they would have by now. This option, though attempted by many, has an extremely high failure rate.
- The second option used most often is the take-over. In this situation, the church taking over generally has the church being taken over vacate all leadership positions. The property is deeded over, and the older church ceases to exist.

This is the option used most often by FBCW. FBCW does not seek out the churches to be taken-over. Most often FBCW is asked by the churches to consider taking them over. FBCW then provides fresh vision from fresh leadership. The church begins to re-engage the community.

FBCW has seen a significant degree of success with this process over the past several years. Churches on the brink of death with little or no resources have turned around and become very strong churches. The churches are provided with a campus pastor who handles the day-to-day operation of the church as well as the local ministries.

- The third option involves a consultation with the revitalization church. The data gleaned from the research project has helped this process more than any other. I have used the things learned in the research project with revitalization churches to a great degree of success.

One of the biggest issues with revitalization churches involves why the church declined. The next biggest issue involves what the church will do now to address the issues. The key components discovered in the research project also apply to revitalization churches. The key components of enhanced predictability of success have been missing in the revitalization churches with which I have worked.

The field of revitalization has only a few processes available to assist in seeing the church become vibrant again. The data utilized from the research project allows another field-tested and proven methodology to be used and implemented. The evaluation of the benefit to revitalization churches has been realized.

Evaluation: Have the Key Components Been Identified and Proven to Be Effective for Church Plants and Revitalization Churches?

The key components leading to enhanced predictability were identified in data gathered in the research project. The key components proved to be attainable but not naturally occurring. Churches that succeeded utilized the key components, and churches that did not succeed did not have the key components in their church.

I have taken what has been learned in the research project and utilized it to help churches in revitalization begin to turn around and regain effectiveness. In each case, understanding which of the key components were not present allowed an early conclusion to be drawn about what to do next. As the key components were assembled in the revitalization churches, they gained strength and began to turn around.

Next Steps...What Now?

The research project has been conducted and conclusions have been drawn. The field tests over the past ten months have been completed, the implications noted. The evaluations have been cited, and the book has been written.

What are the next steps in this process? What will happen now that the data has been collected, analyzed, tested, and implemented on a small scale? What effect will *"The Predictability Factor"* have going forward?

Several possibilities exist for utilizing the research project to the fullest:

- Personally, I will continue to implement the key components in church plants and revitalization churches. I will continue to field-test the lessons learned. I will continue to seek ways to make the church planting and revitalization processes of FBCW more effective in incorporating the key components.
- Professionally, I would like to see the key components and the lessons learned and shared in *"The Predictability Factor"* become widely understood and incorporated into church plants and churches in revitalization across America. I would like to see more people confidently answer God's call to be a church planter. I would like to see more churches become involved in church planting, knowing the "risk" has been greatly reduced.
- Spiritually, I would like to see God's kingdom expanded in a significant way. I would like to see churches come back to life. I would like to see churches birthed in strength, not in a survival mode.

Is it possible to see all the things listed here come to fruition? I believe it is, but if not, I have benefitted greatly from the time and interaction with church planters in the field, as well as field-testing the revitalization process. The ministry I am blessed to have has been strengthened and has a bright future. I thank the Lord for what he has done and what he will do in the days ahead.

INDEX

D

E

F

strength, 25–26, 28, 35, 106–7
stress, 62
support, xiv, 12, 36, 50–51, 59, 74, 77,
    80–82, 84
system, xvii, 54, 69, 72

T

theology, 75
time, xiv–xv, xix, 4, 6, 8, 10, 12–17, 28,
    33, 45–46, 61–63, 72–74, 80,
    95–97, 99–100
tool, 9, 11, 26, 49, 53, 72

V

vision, 6–7, 25–28, 30–33, 36–39, 44,
    55, 57–59, 83–84, 87, 94–95,
    97–98, 100, 103

clear, 25, 27–28, 58
defined, xv, 38
fresh, xvi–xvii, 10, 105
visionary, xix

W

Wesleyan Methodist Church, 12
Westbrook, Jeremy, 23, 31, 36–37, 52
whatever-it-takes mentality, xvii–xviii
Woodstock, ix, 16, 35–36, 38, 41, 44,
    47, 59, 81, 103
Woodstock Church Planting School, 35,
    59

NOTES: THE PREDICTABILITY FACTOR

Adams, Dennis. Founder and Pastor, The Church @ Arrowhead, Glendale, AZ.

Agee, Bill. *Church Planting: This is NOT a Manual.* Canton, GA: MarkIV Church Solutions, 2011.

————. *Strategic Focus Cities Initiatives: Phoenix, Arizona, The Whole Story.* 1st ed. Phoenix, AZ, 2001

Baird, Ted. Founder and Pastor, Fellowship Church@ Anthem, Anthem, AZ.

Barley, Bryan. Founder and Pastor, Summit Church, Denver, CO.

Belflower, Ken. State Church Planting Director, Arizona Southern Baptist Convention, Phoenix, AZ.

Browning, Will. Founder and Pastor, Journey Church, Summerville, SC.

Gallaty, Robby. *Growing Up: How to be a Disciple Who Makes Disciples.* Bloomington: Crossbooks, 2013.

Gross, Dale. Founder and Pastor, Northern Hills Church, Phoenix, AZ.

Lashey, Mark. Founder and Pastor, Life House Church, Middletown, DE.

Murray, Stuart. *Church Planting: Laying Foundations.* Scottsdale PE; Waterloo, ON: Herald Press, 2001.

Patton, Monty.   Founder and Pastor, Mountain Ridge Church, Glendale, AZ.

Stetzer, Ed. *North American Mission Board: Church Planting Study.* Alpharetta, GA: North American Mission Board, 2004.

Warren, Rick. *The Purpose Driven Church*, 1st ed. Grand Rapids: Zondervan, 1995.

Westbrook, Jeremy.   Founder and Pastor, Living Hope Church, Marysville, OH.

Printed in the United States
By Bookmasters